S0-BRT-037

The Right to Die

THE
RIGHT
TO
DIE

ELAINE LANDAU

An Impact Book
Franklin Watts
New York/Chicago/London/Toronto/Sydney

FOR
Nancy Lee Plotts

Photographs copyright © : UPI/Bettmann Newsphotos: pp. 1, 2, 3, 15, 16 top; Zephyr Pictures: pp. 4, 6, 8, 9, 10, 11, 12 (all Melanie Carr), 16 bottom (J.K. Hall); Tom Stack & Associates/ David C. London: p. 5; Gamma-Liaison/Detroit News/GP: p. 7; Terry Wild Studios: pp. 13, 14.

Library of Congress Cataloging-in-Publication Data

Landau, Elaine.
    The right to die / Elaine Landau.
        p.   cm.—(Impact)
    Includes bibliographical references and index.
    Summary: Examines the hotly debated question of a terminally ill person's right to die.
    ISBN 0-531-13015-0
    1. Terminal care—Moral and ethical aspects. 2. Right to die. [1. Terminal care—Moral and ethical aspects. 2. Right to die.] I. Title.
R726.L36   1993
174' .24—dc20   93-10800 CIP AC

Contents

The Right to Die

Life and Death

The trouble began early one morning in May 1991. Domenic Ponzo, an East Boston resident, was awakened by a severe pain in his side. He went to a nearby clinic where he was told that the problem stemmed from his gall bladder. Shortly afterwards, he was admitted to a hospital.

Unfortunately, Ponzo's condition rapidly deteriorated. His gall bladder proved to be gangrenous and had to be removed. His kidneys also stopped functioning, and he experienced difficulty breathing on his own. The situation worsened when he suffered a heart attack following the gall bladder surgery.

As the days passed, the hospital's intensive care staff knew that their patient was not going to recover. Ponzo's kidney dialysis had to be stopped since it adversely affected his heart; toxic wastes continued to flood his system. His lungs weren't functioning properly, and he drifted in and out of consciousness.

If the hospital did not intervene with extraordinary measures, Mr. Ponzo was likely to live for another forty-eight hours. If it resorted to massive or *heroic* intervention, including ventilator breathing, continual electric shocks to keep his heart pumping, and extensive drug therapy, Mr. Ponzo might last a week.

In trying to determine how to proceed, the doctors discussed treatment alternatives with Adeline Ponzo, Domenic's sixty-seven-year-old wife. Explaining the hopelessness of the situation, they advised against heroic intervention, which they believed would only prolong the patient's dying.

It was difficult for Mrs. Ponzo to face the negative choices presented. After initially being assured that letting her husband go was the wisest decision, she had replied: "It may be [right] for you, doctor, but he's all I have."[1] However, after fully contemplating the matter, she agreed that letting him go was best.

The following morning Domenic Ponzo fleetingly regained consciousness. During his last moments he and Adeline recalled how wonderful their years together had been. Mrs. Ponzo described their parting this way: "I just held him in my arms. I took off his (oxygen) mask—he didn't need it anymore—and held him and held him until his final breath."[2] The hospital staff later described Mr. Ponzo's passing as a "peaceful death."

Finding a humane and sensible approach to treating the terminally ill has become a hotly debated topic in recent years. The development of advanced life support systems presently permits doctors to keep a patient breathing who, in the past, could not have survived. Yet a segment of our society has increasingly questioned the quality of life afforded these individuals who have sometimes been referred to as the "living dead." Is the medical field's embrace of high technology sustaining life or merely prolonging death?

Dr. Scott Weiss of Boston's Beth Israel Hospital has described "sticking needles in" and "thumping on [the] chest" of a terminally ill patient about to die as "a violent and brutal way to depart this world. You have a responsibility not to drag out the dying," he noted. "I don't believe in euthanasia [mercy killing]. But I don't think we are here to do things that are inappropriate. Some doctors think that once you invoke the high tech, you can't get off the train, but you ought to be able to opt out."[3]

Lynn Kroger's family knows the ramifications of the other alternative all too well. At eighty-two, Mrs. Kroger's father, Edward Winter, had some very definite ideas about health care. The previous October he had lost his wife of fifty-five years after nursing her through a prolonged illness. It had been a difficult time for everyone close to the aging couple. The medical procedures and pain endured by the elderly woman seemed endless, and her husband never wanted his family put through that ordeal again. Since his own health was poor, Mr. Winter saw "no point in being resuscitated" if his condition worsened.

But that's not the way things turned out. While at a senior center, Mr. Winter collapsed and was taken to a hospital. Upon regaining consciousness, he told the staff that if he deteriorated, he did not want to be kept alive. His family also spoke with the physician to underscore Mr. Winter's wishes. Accordingly, the doctor put the instructions, *No Code Blue* (do not resuscitate), on the elderly gentleman's chart.

Yet when the patient had a heart attack the following night, the instructions were ignored. Instead, the doctors present intervened to save Mr. Winter, and before long he resumed breathing on his own. When the elderly patient realized what had transpired, he was furious. He had been kept alive when that wasn't what he had wanted.

Edward Winter's original instructions were repeated, but again unheeded, when thirty hours later he suffered a massive stroke. The stroke was devastating. He was left paralyzed on his right side, incontinent, and experienced difficulty speaking. Twice Mr. Winter had been *saved* against his wishes and as a result, his life was now filled with discomfort and frustration. As his daughter, Mrs. Kroger, described the predicament: "It was so difficult to try to make other people understand what he was going through; I mean, he is—he's so depressed. He is so unhappy. He is so sad. This could have been avoided if they just hadn't, you know, shocked his heart against his wishes. It's ridiculous. It's his right to choose that."[4]

As a result of his experience, Edward Winter decided to protest the injustice and indignity he had been put through. While hospitals had previously been sued for allowing patients to die, Mr. Winter sued the facility for saving his life against his will. William Knapp, his attorney, characterized the thrust of his client's case as follows:

> . . . *The be-all and end-all of being an American citizen is the right to self-determination. The beginning point for any medical decision is informed consent . . . [but] informed consent is meaningless if one doesn't have the right to refuse treatment. This is no different than if you come down with cancer, and your doctor said, "I think you should have chemotherapy," and he put you down on the floor, put his knee on your chest*

and shoved a needle in your arm. That would be
an outrageous situation, and you wouldn't stand
for it. That's basically what happened to Mr.
Winter.[5]

The ultimate decision in treating hopelessly ill people should ideally rest with both the patients or their families (if they are unable to speak for themselves) and the physician handling the case. However, traditionally, most patients tended to passively accept their doctor's dictates in such matters. Due to their extensive training and esteemed position, many physicians comfortably made life and death decisions for their patients. Some justified their actions, arguing that it was often too difficult for a person not medically trained to understand the various effects of a disease and the highly complex treatment alternatives. They also stressed that at times an ill individual's emotional state might interfere with sound decision-making.

Often physicians, therefore, ended up doing everything in their power to save the patient. At times such measures entailed keeping the patient alive sustained by machines and tubes with little hope for recovery. Some doctors have been particularly emphatic about doing what they feel is best for their patients who are not terminally ill but have been handicapped or somewhat physically diminished by an illness or accident and no longer wish to live. These physicians believe that the patient may be basing his or her decision on a distorted view of what it is like to be seriously handicapped. Doctors also stress that rehabilitative medicine has rapidly advanced, and today's medical consequences may not necessarily be tomorrow's.

However, in recent times, many individuals have become knowledgeable about medical issues and

1. *The patient has the right to considerate and respectful care.*

2. *The patient has the right to obtain from his physician complete current information concerning his diagnosis, treatment and prognosis in terms the patient can be reasonably expected to understand. When it is not medically advisable to give such information to the patient, the information should be made available to an appropriate person in his behalf. He has the right to know by name the physician responsible for coordinating his care.*

3. *The patient has the right to receive from his physician information necessary to give informed consent, prior to the start of any procedure and/or treatment. Except in emergencies, such information for informed consent should include but not necessarily be limited to the specific procedure and/or treatment, the medically significant risks involved, and the probable duration of incapacitation. Where medically significant alternatives for care or treatment exist, or when the patient requests information concerning medical alternatives, the patient has the right to such information. The patient also has the right to know the name of the person responsible for the procedures and/or treatment.*

4. *The patient has the right to refuse treatment to the extent permitted by law, and to be informed of the medical consequences of his action.*

5. *The patient has the right to every consideration of his privacy concerning his own medical care program. Case discussion, consultation, examination, and treatment are confidential and should be conducted discreetly. Those not directly involved in his care must have the permission of the patient to be present.*

16

6. *The patient has the right to expect that all communications and records pertaining to his care should be treated as confidential.*

7. *The patient has the right to expect that within its capacity a hospital must make reasonable response to the request of a patient for services. The hospital must provide evaluation, service, and/or referral as indicated by the urgency of the case. When medically permissible a patient may be transferred to another facility only after he has received complete information and explanation concerning the needs for and alternatives to such a transfer. The institution to which the patient is to be transferred must first have accepted the patient for transfer.*

8. *The patient has the right to obtain information as to any relationship of his hospital to other health care and educational institutions insofar as his care is concerned. The patient has the right to obtain information as to the existence of any professional relationships among individuals, by name, who are treating him.*

9. *The patient has the right to be advised if the hospital proposes to engage in or perform human experimentation affecting his care or treatment. The patient has the right to refuse to participate in such research projects.*[9]

The purpose of this document was to reinforce the ill person's rights and sense of control in an atmosphere where he or she may at times feel overwhelmed by a bureaucratic and often impersonal hospital environment. A second intent was to underscore to doctors the importance of patient input in devising a treatment plan.

Nevertheless, a segment of the population feels that even with the Patient's Bill of Rights there is still no guarantee that their doctor will respect their wishes. As a professor at Manhattan's Columbia College of Physicians and Surgeons explained, "There has been an extraordinary decline in trust between physicians and patients and patients and hospitals. People don't believe that the hospital will do what they want."[10] This is especially important at a time when many people appear increasingly prepared to accept the inevitability of death in terminally ill patients. A 1990 Gallup Poll revealed that 84 percent of Americans would opt to discontinue life-support measures if there was no chance of recovery.

While some doctors believe that a peaceful passing is preferable to perhaps inadvertently prolonging a patient's discomfort and death, others still grapple with the moral and legal ramifications of the issue. Terminating treatment when the patient might possibly be sustained for weeks, days, or even hours longer is extremely uncomfortable for some physicians who have consistently viewed themselves as healers. As a Portland, Maine, surgeon who has served as vice chairman of the American Medical Association's board of Trustees put it, "Our social contract is to sustain life and relieve suffering. But sometimes these ideals are in conflict."[11]

There are also less noble but perhaps more practical reasons why some physicians are hesitant to withdraw life supports. Although the patient may genuinely want his or her life to end, the family may strongly disagree with those wishes. At times, doctors wishing to follow their patient's orders have subsequently been threatened with law suits by families claiming that their ill relative was not in the proper state of mind to make such a decision.

In other instances, physicians resort to extraordinary measures because they feel pressured to do everything possible for their patient so as not to appear uncaring or irresponsible. Some doctors also commonly rely on heroic intervention to maintain a knowledgeable image within the hospital community. They may be concerned that foregoing a diagnostic test or not employing high-tech equipment may make them seem behind the latest medical advances.

Those against the arbitrary use of heroic measures argue that presently doctors run the risk of turning into technicians who run machines without regard for the quality of life they sustain. This faction further stresses that we must respect the rights and wishes of the terminally ill and come to grips with death and our feelings about letting go.

But there are other factors involved too. It has been argued that an ill person's wish to die may not always be voluntarily motivated. Not wanting to bankrupt the family with the skyrocketing costs of high-tech medicine or put them through the emotional turmoil often associated with a terminally ill loved one, the patient may opt to do what he or she believes will be the most expedient for the family rather than what he or she might genuinely want to do.

There are also undeniable drawbacks to declaring treatment procedures in advance. As an ethicist at George Washington University succinctly put it, "It's ridiculous to think that you can anticipate the course of an illness decades later."[12] A case in point is that of an eighty-year-old woman from Long Island, New York, who had always stated that she didn't want to be placed on a life support system if she ever became too ill to exist on her own. Unfortunately, following a cerebral hemorrhage, she slipped into a coma. Remembering the woman's often repeated instructions and believing her condition was irreversible, her family and physicians were about to terminate her life supports when she unexpectedly regained consciousness.

Similar situations have occasionally occurred in hospitals across the country. Perhaps the best known such case is that of a Baltimore, Maryland, woman named Jacqueline Cole. At one time Jackie Cole had what many considered an enviable life. Friends and family members often described her as a lively and creative individual. She worked full-time as a teacher-certification officer at the Maryland State Department of Education in addition to counseling students at Johns Hopkins University several hours a week. She was an outstanding artist excelling in both oil portraits and photography as well as a superb cook. In fact, every Friday evening Mrs. Cole baked a dozen cakes for an exclusive area restaurant.

But all that changed one Saturday morning in April 1986. Mrs. Cole, along with three of her four children, was chatting in the family room when she suddenly felt a searing pain in her head that caused her to double over. Claiming that she had just gotten the worst headache she ever had, seconds later Mrs. Cole couldn't feel her arm. It was then that the forty-four-year-old woman realized that she was having a stroke. Her children called for an ambulance, but by the time the emergency medics arrived, Jacqueline Cole was unconscious.

Mrs. Cole's husband, Harry, a Presbyterian minister, later arrived at the hospital to find his wife lying on a hospital gurney attached to an assortment of machines. She had had a cerebral hemorrhage and the doctors felt certain that there was brain damage. The once vibrant woman now lay in a coma unable to breathe without a respirator. Her family was told that she probably wouldn't live through the day. Jackie Cole survived, but her condition stayed the same.

The patient remained hooked up to an array of life-sustaining apparatus, while friends and family members visited and prayed for her recovery. However, Mrs. Cole's medical condition continued to deteriorate. She developed pneumonia along with a serious lung infection and underwent a tracheotomy to assist her breathing. The situation worsened after she went into cardiac arrest.

After about three weeks, the attending physician informed the family that Mrs. Cole was in a persistent vegetative state—she would either die within a short period of time or remain as she was for months or years. The Coles were forced to consider the available options and think about what Jackie would have wanted for herself. She had watched her own mother die as a result of a brain tumor and had insisted that she never wanted to be kept alive by machines. Jackie's daughter recalled that her mother had repeated this just before slipping into the coma.

After discussing the matter as a family, the Coles decided that Jackie's high-tech life supports should be withdrawn. But when her husband spoke to the doctor about it, he was told that he needed a court order. The case was heard on May 9, 1986, by Judge John Carrol Byrnes. The judge listened attentively as the doctor provided the medical data on the patient and the family's attorney argued to discontinue Jacqueline Cole's life supports.

To the family's disappointment, the judge denied their petition. It had only been forty-one days since Jackie Cole had lapsed into the coma, and he felt it was too soon to give up hope. Frustrated by the court's decision, Jackie's husband stood at his wife's bedside and, with tears in his eyes, told her how sorry he was to have failed her. As expected, his comatose spouse made no reply.

Yet within a week the couple was grateful for the verdict. Six days later, John Evans, a close family friend, stopped by the hospital to see how Jackie was doing and offer Harry his support. He gently took the comatose patient's hand and whispered, "Hi, Jackie." To their amazement, at that moment Jacqueline Cole opened her eyes and looked directly at her husband standing at the foot of the bed. Shocked at his wife's surprise reawakening, Harry Cole joyously embraced and kissed the woman he thought would never recognize him again. She smiled broadly and kissed him back. Jackie Cole was obviously glad to be alive.

Jacqueline Cole eventually returned home, and although she experienced some memory loss and needed physical therapy, she now enjoys a happy and fulfilling life with her family. "Miracles can and do occur," her husband remarked. "I guess we've muddied the waters surrounding the question of a person's right to die."[13]

Other important concerns have been raised with regard to the right to die as well. While those who favor allowing hopelessly ill individuals to die without heroic measures view it as a humane option, others believe it brings our society one step closer to what some ethicists have referred to as "institutional heartlessness." The potential for abuse in such situations is vast. Since it annually costs taxpayers over $150,000 to keep an individual on life supports, money could dangerously factor into a medical evaluation. Might some people deem open heart surgery for young children with an excellent chance for survival a wiser expenditure of our limited health care resources than prolonging the existence of comatose elderly patients? Yet can we ever morally afford to put a price tag on anyone's life?

Will individuals less valued by society eventually be more readily eased into a quick *peaceful* death? Might standards established for the right to die ultimately affect countless individuals suffering from dementia (senility), mental retardation, and AIDS?

Critics of the right-to-die stress that even now under the hodgepodge of policies and regulations presently operating in various hospitals and nursing homes, life-support systems have been withdrawn from patients with the potential to live years longer. This occurs despite the fact that a significant number of these individuals are lucid. As attorney Thomas Marzan of the National Legal Center for the Medically Dependent and Disabled described the situation, "People who are not dying are being denied treatment. The family doesn't object, the doctor doesn't object, and no one seems to care." [14] If such practices were undertaken under the "right-to-die" banner, it might become socially acceptable to simply rid society of the unwanted and burdensome sick.

Those who believe in the right to die view "death with dignity" as an important aspect of life. Opponents contend that the true motivation behind these decisions is always questionable and that the process could open a Pandora's box of abuses. It is an emotionally charged issue around which debate is likely to continue.

2

It's What She Would Have Wanted—Or Is It?

Should a hopelessly ill individual's wish to "pull the plug" always be respected? Under some circumstances, the situation becomes extremely complex. What if the person became unconscious prior to either expressing his or her feelings in writing or ever discussing the matter with an attorney or clergy member? What if the person never actually expressed this desire to family or friends, but they feel the person would have wanted it that way? Perhaps someone even recalls the individual saying so after reading about such a case in the newspaper. But should the decision to terminate life-sustaining equipment rest only on the assumptions of those who knew the person? Or on an opinion he or she might have held before becoming ill?

One such case which captured the media's attention a number of years ago was that of twenty-one-year-old Karen Ann Quinlan. On the night of April 15, 1975, Ms. Quinlan was rushed to Newton Memorial Hospital in Newton, New Jersey, when she was found unconscious in her room after having unintentionally consumed a lethal combination of drugs and alcohol.

By the time she arrived at the hospital, the young woman was blue and lifeless. She had no pulse for at least fifteen minutes—perhaps even longer. The medics on the ambulance crew had tried unsuccessfully to revive her en route. After being given oxygen, Ms. Quinlan's color returned somewhat, but extensive brain damage had already occurred.

Since the young woman experienced difficulty breathing at the hospital, the doctors immediately put her on a respirator to keep her alive. Medical experts later reviewing the case agreed that the doctors acted appropriately. At the time, they knew nothing of the new patient's medical history, the substances she had ingested, or the extent of her brain damage.

The medical staff worked to keep Karen Ann Quinlan alive until she was later transferred to St. Clare's Hospital in nearby Denville, New Jersey. There physicians continued to use heroic measures to maintain the life of the young woman for over a year. During that period, her weight dropped to only seventy pounds and she remained comatose in almost a fetal position. The physicians said that she would never see, speak, hear, or respond to those around her again. They thought that if the mechanical respirator had not been turned on when she initially arrived at Newton Memorial Hospital, she might have died that night. Karen Ann's brain was so severely damaged that doctors doubted whether the respirator could regulate her breathing.

Karen's parents, Joe and Julia Quinlan, visited their daughter regularly at St. Clare's. They would talk to her, kiss her brow, and massage her limbs. Each time they came, they hoped that somehow Karen would respond—but she never did. Slowly, the Quinlans concluded that it was pointless and cruel for the young woman to remain on the respirator. As her father stated, "I'm sure that with that mechanism [the respirator] she would continue in the state she's in, but that's not really living. She's just a vegetable."[1]

Mrs. Quinlan continued, "But you know, when you visit her every day . . . you realize that there's absolutely no hope at all. And then you realize that it's best if God just takes her."[2]

The Quinlans eventually went to court to have their daughter taken off the respirator. Their legal battle snowballed into one of the most publicized trials in our nation's history. The family's personal tragedy mirrored the societal schism on an issue affecting countless Americans as medical technology continued to outpace itself.

The case was more involved than it first appeared. Karen Ann was over twenty-one, but she had never left any written or oral directives alluding to the discontinuation of life supports if she was in an irreversible coma. That meant that the court had to base its decision on what those closest to her felt she would have wanted. But critics wondered whether anyone could ever really be certain of another person's unexpressed wishes on this or any matter.

Despite their moving pleas and testimony stating that Karen Ann would not have wanted to live out her life on a respirator, the New Jersey Superior Court denied the Quinlans' petition. However, the family appealed the verdict, and on April 1, 1976, almost a full year after Karen Ann slipped into the coma, the New Jersey Supreme Court reversed the lower court's decision. It ruled that life supports could be withdrawn from a patient in a comatose state if there was no chance of recovery, and it was clear that the patient would not want to have remained indefinitely on life supports. The court further determined that no one (neither the hospital personnel nor the family) could be held civilly or criminally liable in such instances.

In support of the decision, New Jersey Supreme Court Justice Richard J. Hughes noted that a number of physicians testified that they had "refused to inflict an undesired prolongation of the process of dying on a patient in irreversible condition when it is clear that such 'therapy' offers neither human or humane benefit." The judge added, "We think these attitudes represent a balanced implementation of a profoundly realistic perspective in the meaning of life and death and that they respect the whole Judeo-Christian tradition of regard for human life."[3]

It looked as though the Quinlans' ordeal was finally over, but it actually wasn't. The physicians caring for Karen Ann at St. Clare's labeled the court decision unmerciful and stressed that as doctors they would abide by the "irreversible tenet to protect life." Although they took Karen Ann off the respirator, she was put in a private room where, for over two months, she received an extraordinary degree of care including twenty-four hour a day nurses, nutritious high calorie tubal feedings, high doses of antibiotics and other drugs, and continual massages. While she never emerged from her coma, Karen Ann Quinlan did what no one had expected her to do—she lived.

After over two months of intensive care, Karen Ann's doctors publicly announced that they could not morally allow their patient to die at St. Clare's. Although comatose, they claimed that she was healthy. However, Karen Ann's *health* was debatable. The Quinlan family, along with many who agreed with them, did not feel that existing in a world without thought and speech—not knowing who you were or who was with you—could ever be con-

withdrawn and his wife could move him to a facility that would cooperate with her request.

Right-to-die advocates applauded the court's decision. However, the case evoked a national controversy over precisely what constitutes an artificial life support. Most people agree that a respirator is a life-sustaining medical tool, but some people feel differently about depriving a hopelessly ill person of food and water. They argue that sustenance is a basic survival need and cannot be regarded as anything less. These individuals stress that when people dine out, they don't equate it with taking a prescription medication or seeing a doctor. Right-to-die opponents feel that starving patients to death is just another way of ridding society of very ill and severely disabled individuals capable of surviving without genuine life supports.

Nevertheless, in recent years, several courts have supported feeding tube removal. In 1986 California resident Elizabeth Bouvia, who had suffered from cerebral palsy, won the right to have her feeding tube withdrawn. The court determined that the issue was actually out of its realm and instead was "a moral and philosophical decision that belongs to the patient alone as a competent adult." Following the legal outcome, however, Bouvia changed her mind, citing that it had been too painful to try to starve herself.

The question was examined in greater depth in the 1990s with the case of Nancy Cruzan. On January 11, 1983, twenty-six year-old Ms. Cruzan had been in a terrible automobile accident on an icy road while driving home from work. Her car had swerved and overturned, and she was later found lying face down in a ditch. Although the paramedics arriving at the scene managed to restart Cruzan's heart, she had stopped breathing for about fifteen minutes and, like Karen Quinlan, had sustained severe brain damage.

For the next eight years, Ms. Cruzan lay quietly in a hospital bed in what her doctors described as an "irreversible vegetative state." As time passed her body stiffened and her arms and legs atrophied. Ms. Cruzan's hands curled under, causing her fingernails to cut into her wrists. At times, the nurses wedged napkins under her fingers to prevent her from piercing the flesh. While it was difficult for them to adjust to their daughter's state, Cruzan's parents accepted that Nancy would never again hug them, laugh with a friend, or play with her nieces. Life as she had known it was over, and the young woman her family loved and enjoyed seemed gone as well.

The young woman's doctors claimed she would never regain consciousness. Yet some hospital nurses reported that Ms. Cruzan occasionally turned toward those who addressed her and that she had even cried a number of times. Once her tears flowed after she was read a touching valentine card. At times, even her parents thought they detected glimpses of awareness in their daughter. Her father said, "Sometimes you swear she is looking right at you, but then you move three or four steps [and you realize she's not]. She has no awareness of herself."[5]

The three doctors caring for Nancy Cruzan as well as several neurologists and a neurosurgeon confirmed that there was no chance of even a partial recovery. Ironically, Ms. Cruzan had survived through the years without a respirator or other complex life-support devices. But since she couldn't swallow, she had a feeding tube.

Claiming that their daughter would have never wanted to live this way, Lester and Joyce Cruzan went before the circuit court of Jasper County, Missouri, to ask that the feeding tube inserted in Nancy's stomach be removed. Judge Charles E. Tell, Jr., ruled in their favor, explaining his decision as follows: "There is a fundamental natural right expressed in our Constitution as to the 'right of liberty' which permits an individual to refuse or to direct the withholding or withdrawal of artificial life-prolonging procedures when a person has no cognitive brain function."[6]

But, like the Quinlans, the family's relief was short-lived. After the state appealed the verdict, the Missouri Supreme Court reversed the lower court, affirming "the sanctity of life." In the decision, Missouri State Supreme Court Justice Edward Robertson stressed that this was not a case of asking the court "to let someone die," but "to allow the medical profession to make Nancy die by starvation and dehydration."

The court further determined that there wasn't any clear and convincing evidence of Nancy Cruzan's desire to end her life or that the feeding tube sustaining her was "heroically invasive or burdensome." The justices added that in instances where a human life hangs in the balance, they "choose to err on the side of life."

Refusing to accept the state supreme court's decision, the Cruzan family's attorneys brought the case before the United States Supreme Court. The outcome would not only affect the Cruzans but would establish future legal guidelines for the plight of thousands of Americans in similar predicaments. The case's ramifications were especially significant considering that one day seven out of ten Americans will either be on life supports or have a loved one on them.

Yet the Cruzan case was complicated on a number of levels. Nancy Cruzan wasn't actually dying.

In fact, her doctors estimated that she could live for at least another thirty years as she was. The physicians also noted that she was not in any pain or discomfort. Instead, it was her parents who suffered. Aware of what Nancy had become and her bleak prognosis, they had to watch their daughter in what they perceived as a living death.

While the debate continued, a segment of the population voiced its sympathy for the Cruzan family. Among their supporters was Pete Busalacchi, whose twenty-year-old daughter Christine was in the same Missouri rehabilitation center as Ms. Cruzan. "I'm riding on the Cruzan's coattails," he remarked in describing his own daughter's condition. "This has been a thirty-four month funeral. . . . My suggestion [to the Cruzans] is to take Nancy to the Supreme Court and wheel her in and ask, 'Do you want to live like this?' " [7]

Despite the outpouring of sympathy, the Cruzans' request to have their daughter's feeding tube removed raised ethical issues that could not be ignored. As University of Michigan law professor Yale Kamisar stated, "Whose rights are being fought for, Nancy Cruzan's or her parents? Whose preferences are being achieved?" [8] There was also the more basic issue of condoning the removal of food and water as withdrawing a legitimate medical treatment. Despite the American Medical Association's (AMA) acceptance of this view, many individuals, including some doctors, found it morally repugnant.

As it turned out, the United States Supreme Court decision had an interesting twist. On the one hand, the Court determined that an individual whose wishes are clearly known has a constitutional right not to be subjected to unwanted life supports. It also recognized artificially providing food and water to patients as a medical procedure. However, the jus-

camped outside the hospital to hold a prayer vigil for her.

"It's a shame that as a society we have no more compassion for the helpless than to starve them when they become useless to us," noted Rev. Joseph Foreman, who had been among the protestors. "There were hundreds of bona fide offers to care for her, and they were rejected in favor of starving her to death. She was not given the legal protection that a criminal [would have been given]."[12] Another demonstrator remarked that although Nancy Cruzan once cared for severely disabled children, when she was unable to care for herself, no one was there for her.

Although some people view Nancy's death as an act of mercy, others believe it was merely killing for convenience. Since it's now up to the states to determine how to apply the "right to die" standard in individual cases, there is bound to be a good deal of variation in how these matters are handled. Social critics suspect that in the future, families of hopelessly ill patients unable to meet one state's requirements to terminate life supports will move their relatives to an area with less stringent specifications. As University of Missouri ethicist William Bondeson described the phenomenon, "I tell my students to buy stock in moving companies. This will happen again and again."[13]

3

Advance Directives for Health Care

At age eighty-five, Estelle Browning of Dunedin, Florida, had seen enough hopelessly ill friends to know that she did not want her life prolonged by machines if she were unable to speak for herself. To make sure that never occurred, Ms. Browning filled out a document known as a living will, clearly spelling out her health care wishes. In precisely listing the medical procedures she didn't want, Mrs. Browning rejected the use of a feeding tube. She wrote, "I do not desire that nutrition and hydration be provided by gastric tube or intravenously."[1] Once the documents were in order, the elderly woman breathed a sigh of relief. She told her friends, "Thank God, I can go in peace when my time comes."

But Estelle Browning wasn't able to do that after all. In 1986, the following year, she suffered a cerebral hemorrhage, resulting in permanent brain damage. Although her doctors saved her life, friends who saw Ms. Browning afterwards realized that she was just a shadow of her former self, exhibiting only fleeting signs of consciousness. The physicians inserted a feeding tube into Ms. Browning's abdomen, and when her condition stabilized, they transferred her to a nursing home for long-term care.

Although in her living will Estelle Browning asked not to have a feeding tube, the health care facility claimed that her request could not be honored due to a state regulation requiring nursing homes to feed all patients. In addition, Florida law did not recognize a patient's right to refuse food and water.

Mrs. Browning was forced to remain as she was even though she had tried to take precautions against this. The annual cost of her care was over $36,000, and outside of the small percentage paid by Medicare, the money was systematically withdrawn from her personal assets. Estelle Browning did not have a large family to come to her aid. She was a widow, and her only child had been killed on the battleship *Arizona* when Japan attacked Pearl Harbor during World War II. But, fortunately, a second cousin agreed to act as her court-appointed guardian in a legal effort to have Mrs. Browning's feeding tube removed in accordance with her wishes.

However, a court dispute arose over the interpretation of the term "imminent death." Mrs. Browning's living will specified that heroic measures should be stopped once death was imminent—a condition which her guardian felt had been met. Yet a Florida court determined that Estelle Browning's death was not imminent, since she could be sustained indefinitely by the feeding tube. The case was slated to be heard later by Florida's Supreme Court, but meanwhile Estelle Browning was left in a medical and legal no man's land.

State laws on living wills differ significantly, and in some areas, such as Florida, safeguards originally designed to protect the individual sometimes contradict a patient's final wishes or what may actually be in his or her best interests. Mrs. Browning's attorney, George Felos, expressed the essence of his client's plight: "The standard should not be whether she [Mrs. Browning] could live on the feeding tube, but how long she would live without it."[2]

As time passed, Estelle Browning's condition deteriorated. Despite medical efforts to keep her alive, she died in July 1991, nearly five years after she initially lost consciousness. Two months after her death, Florida's Supreme Court ruled that living will provisions must be honored by health care facilities throughout the state. While the verdict brought welcome relief to other Florida patients in similar predicaments, it came too late for Estelle Browning.

Although Mrs. Browning's living will did not protect her as she had hoped it would, these documents have been extremely useful to countless other Americans. Since the 1980s, increasing numbers of individuals have expressed the desire to exert some degree of control over their medical treatment if they become unable to make decisions. To ensure that their feelings are known, they complete advance health care directives while they are still competent. An advance directive may be a living will, a durable power of attorney for health care, or a combination of both. These choices are discussed below.

Living Wills

A living will, sometimes referred to as an "instruction directive," specifies an individual's wishes or instructions for health care in advance. Generally, living wills give directions regarding life-prolonging treatments and conditions under which the person would or would not want these treatments carried out. "Life-prolonging" treatments generally include artificial breathing, feeding through tubes, surgical procedures, dialysis, restarting the heart, medications (other than those for comfort), and other treatments.

The first living wills tended to be nonspecific, but were thought sufficient to convey an individual's future health care wishes. A typical one might have been similar to the sample below:

"Should I be in an incurable or irreversible mental or physical condition with no reasonable expectation of recovery, I direct my physician to withhold or withdraw treatment that merely prolongs my dying. I further direct that my treatment be limited to measures to keep me comfortable and to relieve pain."[3]

In practice, these wills often proved problematic for doctors and health care facilities. Accurately discerning a patient's wishes in a crisis was difficult when health care professionals had to decipher such vague terms as "terminally ill," "life-prolonging," and similar wording which frequently surfaced in these documents.

Ambiguous phrases, open to various interpretations, left doctors without a clear notion of which measures were to be stopped, started, or maintained. In numerous instances across the country, physicians continued life supports simply because they feared the courts might not support their interpretation of the patient's instructions. The situation was worsened by the fact that various states often define the general terms used in living wills differently. This is particularly true in instances where a patient is being kept alive through a feeding tube. In states in which artificial feeding is considered a "life-sustaining procedure," the measure can be withdrawn. But in other areas where tubal feeding is not deemed heroic or life-extending, feeding cannot be stopped.

These factors make it especially important when writing a living will to specify which treatments are to be withheld or performed and under what circumstances. It is best to clearly state whether cardiac resuscitation, mechanical respiration, or artificial feeding should be resorted to and, if so, under what conditions. It is also possible to specify if a particular treatment should be tried and discontinued if there is no improvement.

Yet even under the best circumstances, living will problems may arise when the unexpected occurs. For example, a person might have his or her living will state that artificial feeding is not to be instituted if there is no chance of recovery, but may fail to say whether he or she wants antibiotics (a life-extending measure) used to combat pneumonia under the same conditions. In other instances, such as the Browning case previously described, living will specifications may conflict with state laws. If the law further states that life supports may only be withdrawn if the person is terminally ill, these measures will be applied to a comatose person even though that may not be what that person wanted.

Another difficulty with living wills is that it is impossible for anyone to know how he or she will feel once illness becomes a reality. What if at the last minute a patient changes his or her mind, but because the illness makes the patient intermittently delusional, the medical staff adheres to the original terms of the patient's living will?

Despite the flaws and inherent complications of living wills, many medical experts believe a living will at least affords an individual a measure of input. Different forms may be used to create a living will, but all these documents basically have the same intent. A person can either use the form provided by Choice In Dying (see sample on facing page), a form devised by the state in which the person resides, or a similar format of one's choice. Once the living will has been completed, it is best to take the following further precautions:

1. A living will should be signed in front of two witnesses and a notary. Copies should be given to responsible family members, the individual's clergyman, lawyer, or any other person who might be called upon to help interpret the individual's wishes.

2. The individual should discuss the living will with his or her physician. It is important that the doctor understand and support the person's wishes and agree to follow the directives in a medical emergency. If the doctor strongly disagrees with the patient's views in these matters, it might be wise to consider changing physicians. In any case, the physician should not be designated in a living will as a decision maker. The doctor cannot act as proxy and treat the patient at the same time.

3. A living will should be kept in a place where family members or other appropriate people can easily find it. It is not advisable to keep a living will in a safe-deposit box since the ill person may be the only one with access to the key.

4. Living wills should be signed again and dated every two to four years. A living will that has been recently reviewed is more likely to be honored by a physician or judge if there is a controversy.

Through the years, living wills have gained increasing acceptance. In December 1991, a new law went into effect requiring all federally funded hospitals, nursing homes, and hospices to inform incoming patients of the laws in their state regarding living wills and other advance directives for health

Living Will Declaration

INSTRUCTIONS
*Consult this column
for help and guidance.*

To My Family, Doctors, and All Those Concerned with My Care

I, _____, being of sound mind, make this statement as a directive to be followed if I become unable to participate in decisions regarding my medical care.

This declaration sets forth your directions regarding medical treatment.

If I should be in an incurable or irreversible mental or physical condition with no reasonable expectation of recovery, I direct my attending physician to withhold or withdraw treatment that merely prolongs my dying. I further direct that treatment be limited to measures to keep me comfortable and to relieve pain.

You have the right to refuse treatment you do not want, and you may request the care you do want.

These directions express my legal right to refuse treatment. Therefore I expect my family, doctors, and everyone concerned with my care to regard themselves as legally and morally bound to act in accord with my wishes, and in so doing to be free of any legal liability for having followed my directions.

You may list specific treatment you do not want. For example:
Cardiac resuscitation
Mechanical respiration
Artificial feeding/ fluids by tube
Otherwise, your general statement, top right, will stand for your wishes.

I especially do not want: _____
_____
_____
_____
_____
_____
_____
_____
_____
_____
_____

You may want to add instructions for care you do want—for example, pain medication; or that you prefer to die at home if possible.

Other instructions/comments: _____
_____
_____
_____
_____
_____

If you want, you can name someone to see that your wishes are carried out, but you do not have to do this.

Proxy Designation Clause: Should I become unable to communicate my instructions as stated above, I designate the following person to act in my behalf:
Name _____
Address _____
If the person I have named above is unable to act on my behalf, I authorize the following person to do so:
Name _____
Address _____

Signed: _____ Date: _____
Witness: _____ Witness: _____
Address: _____ Address: _____

Sign and date here in the presence of two adult witnesses, who should also sign.

Keep the signed original with your personal papers at home. Give signed copies to doctors, family, and proxy. Review your Declaration from time to time; initial and date it to show it still expresses your intent.

Courtesy of Choice In Dying

care. They are then supposed to help the patient draw up one if he or she wishes to do so. In California, some health care facilities even offer information on living wills in ten different languages.

Durable Power of Attorney

Still another advance directive for health care which can be used in connection with or in place of a living will is a durable power of attorney. Also known as a proxy directive, this document appoints someone to make health care decisions for an individual when that person is no longer able to act on his or her own behalf. A durable power of attorney differs from the standard power of attorney often used in business dealings, in that it does not lapse after a specified period of time or when the person granting it becomes incompetent.

The proxy chosen, usually a friend or family member, should be thoroughly familiar with the person's health care wishes. Ideally, the proxy would make the same health care decisions that the ill individual would make if able to. In selecting a durable power of attorney, it is important to remember that if there's a conflict, a judge is more likely to be persuaded by an impartial friend than a relative who also happens to be the incapacitated person's heir. It is also advisable to designate a back-up person for the task in case the first proxy is unavailable at the time of an emergency.

Perhaps the main advantage to having a durable power of attorney is that the proxy can assist in interpreting the patient's probable wishes if a situation arises that has not been covered in the ill person's living will. The proxy can evaluate various treatment alternatives with the fullest information possible.

Since there are no national laws or guidelines regulating the implementation of advance health care directives, their value and effectiveness continue to vary from state to state. Nevertheless, in an age of growing awareness about medical practices, many people feel that these documents are a positive step in the right direction.

4 Death in the Nursery

In April 1982, a Bloomington, Indiana, couple known only as Mr. and Mrs. Doe to protect their anonymity, eagerly awaited the birth of their third child. Both parents were former school teachers and seemed to genuinely enjoy being around young people. Mrs. Doe previously gave birth to two healthy, normal children, and there was no reason for her obstetrician, Walter Owens, to anticipate a problem birth now.

But on the night of April 9, as Owens delivered the Does' child, he realized that the infant faced disastrous health problems. The six-pound baby was completely limp and had turned blue from oxygen deprivation. The doctor also recognized the signs of Down's syndrome, which meant the baby was mentally retarded. The child's health was further jeopardized, since his esophagus hadn't developed normally, preventing the intake of food and water. His heart was also abnormally enlarged and the doctor suspected that there were other disabilities as well.

The family's pediatrician, Dr. James Schaffer, was immediately called in to consult with the obstetrician. Meanwhile, Dr. Owens told the parents that their child was seriously disabled. Feeling as if their world were about to fall apart, both Mr. and Mrs. Doe began to cry. But there was no time for tears. If Baby Doe was to survive, radical procedures needed to be started immediately. To that end, the physicians discussed various treatment options with the parents.

The pediatrician, Dr. Schaffer, urged the Does to have their son transferred to the James Whitcomb Riley Children's Hospital in Indianapolis where surgery could be performed to open the infant's blocked duodenum. Then the food from his stomach could enter his intestines. Without the operation, the boy would not be able to eat or drink, since the oral intake of food would cause suffocation. Schaffer added that at the children's hospital the baby could undergo a sophisticated battery of diagnostic tests to discover the extent of his other disabilities.

But Dr. Owens, the obstetrician, disagreed with his colleague's recommendation. He reminded the parents that regardless of what was done, the child would still be mentally retarded and seriously disabled. He told them that if, instead, they refused to sign the treatment consent forms, the baby was likely to die within days.

Owens attributed his attitude to an incident that had occurred within his own family. His nephew's wife gave birth to a child with multiple disabilities, and the young couple followed their doctor's directive to authorize immediate surgery. The results were tragically disappointing. The doctor described what happened:

The child has never been normal. It learned to walk at the age of four, and it has never learned to talk. It is, at times, aggressive and destructive. My nephew and his wife are very strong people and have handled it. But they've had no more children. She has essentially devoted her life to caring for this retarded child. Obviously, this has colored my thinking on the survival of such children. I believe there are things worse than having a child die. And one of them is that it might live." [1]

The Does needed some time to decide what was best for their family. For the next twenty minutes, they discussed the choices with their best friends, who had remained in the waiting room. Shortly afterwards, the father announced to the doctors that they would forgo treatment for the child. Dismayed by their decision, Dr. Schaffer tried to make the parents reconsider. When they refused, he became incensed and warned Dr. Owens that he could be charged with criminal liability.

But the Does held firmly to their decision and Owens continued to support them. The child remained in the hospital nursery, where the staff was instructed not to start intravenous feedings. They were also told to keep the baby as comfortable as possible and provide sedation when necessary.

Aware that they were on shaky ground, the Does spoke with an attorney. There had been talk of criminal action earlier, and in the hours that followed, the hospital administrator had urged the parents to take their baby home. When the Does declined to do so, they were made to sign a release relieving the hospital of all responsibility if the infant died.

The hospital's attorney felt the issue might best be resolved through a judicial hearing. That way a judge would either order the Does to send the baby to the Riley Children's Hospital or remove the infant from the hospital. Either way, he hoped culpability for the child's ineffective care would not rest with the medical facility. Due to time restraints, the hearing was held in a makeshift courtroom in the hospital. The doctors spoke, as did the Does' attorney. When they finished, the judge determined that since the medical staff presented the couple with two treatment alternatives, the baby's parents had the right to choose either one.

Baby Doe was permitted to remain in the hospital, but his presence in the special care nursery upset the nurses. Outraged at being expected to ignore the urgent medical needs of a very sick infant, a group of them threatened to walk off the job. They claimed that they had become pediatric nurses to save babies, not to participate in their murder. One nurse described her feelings this way: "Without a doubt, it was the most inhumane thing I've ever been involved in. I had all this guilt just standing by, giving him injections, and doing nothing for him."[2] As a result, the child was taken from the nursery and put in a private room on another floor. The little boy's parents were forced to hire private nurses for him.

As word spread of the judge's decision to allow the child to die, local right-to-life organizers were drawn into the controversy. Criticizing the judge for failing to appoint a guardian ad litem or legal advocate to speak on the child's behalf, they characterized the legal proceedings as biased. In response, the judge appointed the Monroe County Department of Public Welfare guardian ad litem and asked that the department's Child Protection Committee review his decision. After examining the evidence, the committee supported the judge's determination. The Does breathed a sigh of relief, thinking that perhaps the public scrutiny of their very personal ordeal was over.

49

It wasn't. The county prosecutor and his assistant felt that they had witnessed a very frightening turn of events. The two didn't want to see a precedent set whereby parents could sound the death knell for their disabled infants if they didn't feel prepared to care for them. In a last ditch effort to save Baby Doe, the men had the child declared neglected under the state's Child in Need of Services (CHINS) law.

Since time was crucial in this case, a second judicial hearing was immediately called. Once again, those involved presented their viewpoints and another judge reviewed the evidence. As before, the presiding justice found that Mr. and Mrs. Doe hadn't done anything wrong. He wrote, "The court finds that the State has failed to show that this child's physical or mental condition is seriously impaired or seriously endangered as a result of the inability, refusal, or neglect of his parents to supply the child with necessary food and medical care."[3]

Baby Doe's condition was rapidly deteriorating. Without nourishment, his body weight had dropped and the infant cried incessantly. After his stomach acid attacked his lungs, the child had started to spit blood. To make him more comfortable, the nurses massaged his back and limbs and suctioned the blood from his throat. But they were well aware that their tiny patient was dying.

Those who strongly believed that Baby Doe had the right to live refused to give up. Right-to-life attorneys unsuccessfully attempted to get a temporary restraining order so that the child could be fed intravenously while the debate over his treatment continued. A national right-to-life association attorney even entered a petition on behalf of a couple who were willing to adopt Baby Doe despite his disabilities. But the Does' attorney refused the offer, arguing that his clients declined medical treatment for the child not because they wanted to rid themselves of the infant but because they believed it was cruel to force the baby to survive with multiple birth defects.

Still hoping to save Baby Doe, right-to-life attorneys petitioned the Indiana Court of Appeals to hear the case, but it refused. They failed at the state Supreme Court level as well. By now what had happened at Bloomington Hospital had become national news, resulting in some unpleasant consequences for the Does. The couple received threatening phone calls and letters and eventually had to have a guard temporarily stationed outside the front door of their home.

While his fate was debated in the media, Baby Doe lay dying in the hospital. He lost all muscle tone, began hemorrhaging, and, at one point, even stopped breathing. Dr. Schaffer, the pediatrician who had been adamantly opposed to the Does' decision, threatened to begin intravenously feeding the infant despite the court ruling, but he was prevented from doing so. Six days after his birth, Baby Doe died.

The case was over, but the circumstances surrounding his death still exist for countless other infants. The right to die becomes especially difficult when newborns are involved. Unable to speak for themselves, they are involuntarily dependent on their parents and physicians to do the right thing.

At times, though, it is extremely difficult to know what the right thing is. High-tech medicine has invaded hospital nurseries throughout the country with compelling force. Today it is possible for neonatologists (physicians specializing in newborn care) to save premature and extremely ill infants who would have never previously survived. In the past, a baby weighing under 2.2 pounds rarely lived, but today more than half of these children do. In fact, now over 75 percent of the babies born weighing just a pound and a half live.

A high-tech neonatal hospital nursery may seem like a step into the twenty-first century. Rows of babies lay in a warm, seemingly airless, room attached to life-extending tubes and wires. There are machines everywhere with panels equipped with a variety of dials, switches, flashing lights, bobbing needles, and digital monitoring systems. Each breath, heartbeat, and physiological change in these tiny struggling patients is meticulously monitored by nurses twenty-four hours a day.

Even with the best equipment, treating tiny and at times very ill infants is a challenge. It is extremely difficult for a physician to draw blood from a premature baby whose artery is smaller than the needle's tip. Frequently, the medical staff is forced to deal with serious complications such as respiratory failure, brain hemorrhages resulting in mental retardation, congestive heart failure, calcium deficiency, infection, and a host of other negative possibilities.

Although a significant number of infants survive, many are left devastatingly disabled. A Stanford University Hospital follow-up study of sixty infants treated in high-tech neonatal nurseries showed that by age three nearly a third of them had serious disabilities. These included moderate to profound mental retardation, partial or total sensory loss, blindness, deafness, paralysis, and cerebral palsy.

Similarly disturbing research conducted at the Hospital for Sick Children in Toronto, Canada, revealed that out of 158 infants treated in a neonatal unit who had weighed less than 801 grams at birth, 119 died. Three of the survivors were blind, fifteen had speech difficulties, and six suffered from hearing problems. All of the infants with a birthweight of under 700 grams had multiple disabilities.

Such unsettling consequences have resulted in an emotionally charged controversy over whether these infants should always be saved. A case in point is that of a baby named Cara Lynn. Cara Lynn's mother, Mrs. B, claims that early on in her pregnancy she knew that something was wrong, but her obstetrician dismissed her concerns. She thought she was carrying the fetus too low, and when the baby moved it felt as though she were being hit with a flipper rather than an arm.

Nevertheless, her pregnancy proceeded normally until the eighth month when she began to hemorrhage. At that point, Mrs. B's doctor instructed her to go immediately to the hospital for ultrasound testing. The results were disastrous. The baby was severely malformed and not expected to live very long following its birth.

Mrs. B and her husband went home to wait for the arrival of an infant who might either be dead or dying at birth. Unlike other expectant couples, they didn't spend the next few weeks buying baby furniture, toys, or infant wear; instead, they began to mourn for their still unborn child.

Their daughter, Cara Lynn, proved to be anencephalic. This meant that the upper portion of her head was missing. Born without a cerebral cortex, her skull stopped about two inches above her eyes, which were fused shut. The top of the baby's head was covered with a fluid-filled pinkish colored membrane. Cara Lynn also had a cleft palate, unmatched ears that rested lower than usual along the side of her head, and missing fingers as well as some that were fused together. As her mother had suspected, one of Cara Lynn's arms resembled a flipper. There were also problems in the lower portion of the infant's body and extremities. The baby suffered from a deformed hip, a club foot, and malformed toes.

Cara Lynn's parents were warned that the baby was only expected to live for a few days and they were advised not to bond with her. Since it was suggested that they not visit the infant, Mr. and Mrs. B called the hospital every few hours to check on their child.

Cara Lynn fared better in the hospital's high-tech neonatal nursery than expected. Days turned into weeks, and the baby's parents were eventually allowed to bring her home. Yet no one was very optimistic about Cara Lynn's future, since an anencephalic baby had never lived as long as six months.

Caring for the child was difficult and exhausting. The baby's head dressings needed to be changed every two hours, and she was on a three-hour feeding schedule. The diaper changes seemed endless, and Mr. and Mrs. B knew that regardless of how long Cara Lynn lived, their daughter would never be toilet trained.

The task of caring for Cara Lynn fell almost solely on her parents. It was impossible for Mr. and Mrs. B to find babysitters who would take on the physically demanding and emotionally draining chore of looking after a baby like theirs. On a few occasions, the couple managed to engage licensed practical nurses, but each one left after her initial shift, refusing to return.

Cara Lynn lived for longer than anyone anticipated. But, four and a half years later, she still spent her days as she had for most of her young life—lying flat on her back in a wheelchair staring into space. Due to her severe medical problems, she is in pain much of the time.

Mr. and Mrs. B feel that their daughter has more of an existence than a life. Unable to see or think, she has no idea of who she is or who her parents are. The cost of her medical care has been astounding. Some people view Cara Lynn's prolonged life as a neonatal success story. But others feel that her physical suffering and poor quality of life make that a dubious assumption.

Mrs. B stresses that while right-to-life groups fight to save every infant regardless of its condition, they are rarely around to face the consequences. "Where are they?" she asked. "They step into a life, do their thing and good-bye. . . . These people save a life, clap their hands after it's done, and then they turn away."[4]

Cara Lynn's parents love their daughter, but watching her agony and meeting her physical needs have been overwhelming. Her father described how they'll feel when she dies: "It will be very sad and it will be a great relief."[5]

Is saving babies like Cara Lynn a moral and ethical imperative or the mindless result of increasingly sophisticated medical advances? As a country, we are divided on the issue, and the courts have yet to set firm legal guidelines in this area. In fact, few areas of the law are as hazy as that surrounding the question of allowing disabled newborns to die. In theory, denying a sick infant food, water, or medical treatment might be considered homicide, but few parents are ever prosecuted in such cases.

This is generally because the authorities are rarely made aware of instances in which life-extending measures are denied these children. But even in cases where it is deliberately brought to their attention, action is seldom taken against those involved. For example, in the 1970s, when two Yale physicians publicly announced that within a two-year period forty-three infants at the New Haven Hospital died due to the deliberate withholding of life-extending treatment, no grand jury hearing was ever called.

In these situations, conflicting ideologies may come into play. On the one hand, laws exist to protect helpless children from neglect and abuse by their parents or legal guardians. Yet in America, parents have traditionally been given a great deal of latitude in making health care decisions for their offspring. Is it abusive not to treat an infant with disastrous disabilities? Or is it reprehensible to condemn a newborn to a physically and mentally limited life of discomfort?

There are no clear-cut answers, and even though parents and doctors are not usually criminally indicted for letting very ill babies die, at times they have been. One such case occurred in 1981 when Dr. Robert Mueller, his wife, Pamela, and the couple's pediatrician were charged with conspiring to kill the Muellers' Siamese twins, Scott and Jeff. The boys, born joined at the hip, shared a leg, bladder, and bowel. Unfortunately, at their birth, hospital personnel felt that they could not be separated surgically.

The pair was therefore placed in the facility's nursery with the order "Do not feed in accordance with parents' wishes" on their charts. However, nurses caring for the twins couldn't bear to see them slowly starve. They secretly fed the boys as well as anonymously notified child welfare authorities.

Although the Muellers had always been well thought of in the community, the court immediately relinquished their custody of the children and had the welfare department supervise the infants' care. The presiding judge wrote of the case:

The juvenile court must follow the constitution of Illinois and the United States, each of which contains a bill of rights. These bills of rights give even newborn Siamese twins with severe abnormalities the inalienable right to life. Has our society retrograded to the stage where we mortals can say to a newborn abnormal child, "You have no right to try to live with a little help from us. . . ." Anyone . . . unless they have a brick in place of a heart, must have compassion for all involved, but when we put ourselves above the law and our Constitution, we get into trouble.[6]

Shortly thereafter, the county prosecutor filed attempted murder charges against the couple and the obstetrician, arguing that despite the emotional and financial burden of raising disabled children, no one has the right to take their lives. To underscore his position, he told the press:

One could easily imagine the pain of the parents. . . . But you also have to feel sorry for the children, hearing the nurses' statements: How they cried in pain because they were hungry; how the cries dwindled down to whimpers as they were starved to death; how their skin started to wrinkle. . . . These were two infant human beings, that feel things just like any other human being does.[7]

The prosecutor's case eventually fell apart. At a pretrial hearing, the pediatric nurses failed to directly link either the parents or the physician with their instructions not to feed the babies. Even the nurse thought to have taken the order over the phone couldn't accurately recall the details of her conversation with the doctor. As a result, the judge dropped the charges, and although the prosecutor later tried to get a grand jury to indict the three, he was unsuccessful.

The Muellers regained custody of the boys and had them placed at Chicago's Children's Memorial Hospital where they frequently visited the twins. Although some people applauded the legal system for saving the children's lives, others argued that the Muellers were victimized in the name of justice. A doctor who later cared for the children stressed that decisions involving the fate of severely disabled newborns should be left to the parents and doctor. He added, "These decisions are never made lightly by the family, and to publicize it in any way only adds to their tragedy."

Yet on numerous occasions, these cases have reached the courts and captured the public's attention. At times, hospitals have sought court orders to override a family's wishes. In some instances, the hospitals feared lawsuits and/or prosecution for allowing these children to die on their premises. Other times nurses, who were right-to-life proponents, reported doctors and parents who quietly conspired to withhold treatment.

In these instances, there is often a difference of opinion within the community as to what is truly best for the child.

As increasing numbers of once unsavable babies are rescued, the gap threatens to widen.

5 Teenagers and the Right to Die

In our society, adults generally make health care choices for minors regardless of the young person's age. Legally responsible for their well-being, parents are expected to act wisely in situations where teenagers are not considered mature enough to actively participate. But what if the patient is a thoughtful older adolescent who just happens to be under eighteen? Should exceptions sometimes be made in health care situations involving life or death choices?

The dilemma reflects concerns apparent in other areas of our society as well. It is difficult to pinpoint precisely when an adolescent should assume adult responsibilities. The legal drinking age has been raised to twenty-one in all fifty states, yet eighteen year olds can go off to war and make crucial life or death battlefield decisions. A recent California law holds parents responsible for atrocities committed by their offspring as gang members; in other states, juveniles charged with particularly heinous murders may be tried as adults.

The ages at which young people can legally marry or independently receive health care reveal similar

59

variations. In many instances, the gulf between law and reality has grown wider as adolescents increasingly participate in activities formerly reserved for adults. Perhaps now more than in the past significant numbers of teenagers are living on their own, holding down jobs, having sex, bearing children, and becoming involved in alcohol and drug use. While many of these behaviors are undesirable, they nevertheless have health care ramifications and raise important questions about adolescent care in medical facilities.

Should an older teen who has largely taken control of his life be treated like a child when serious medical concerns arise? To some extent, that is what happened to Juan (not his real name), an intelligent, mature seventeen year old from Argentina, who was flown to New York for health care.

It wasn't the first time Juan had made the trip. Four years earlier, at age thirteen, Juan had been operated on for a life-threatening brain tumor. Now the problem had resurfaced, and once again the doctors felt that without surgery Juan would die. Juan's mother had researched the treatment alternatives and was anxious for her son to be operated on. But Juan felt differently. Although the young man enjoyed life, he had endured horrendous pain and a difficult recovery period following his last surgery. He had also had to deal with the continual threat of a recurrence during the last four years, and at this point he wasn't willing to go through it all again.

The seventeen year old begged his mother and the doctors to forgo the surgery. He knew that meant that he might die, but he was willing to accept that consequence. Juan felt that at least the time he had left would be bearable.

Although they were moved by his plea to be left

alone, the young man's mother, along with the medical staff, felt that they knew best. As a medical ethicist later described what happened to Juan, "(Juan) was dragged, literally kicking and screaming, into surgery. There was to be no happy ending, unfortunately; he came out of the operation totally insensate (showing a lack of sense or reason) and died four agonizing months later."[1]

Juan's fate raised a host of ethically perplexing questions. Were the physicians involved wrong to ignore the seventeen year old's pleas? Having had the operation before, Juan probably had the best sense of what he would have to endure even if the surgery were successful. With this knowledge, should his thoughts, feelings, and preferences have been disregarded simply because he was still a minor? Should a mother's treatment choice be followed even if an adolescent patient is adamantly opposed to it? Did the doctors go along with the mother's decision because it reinforced their own opinion? If Juan had been just a few months older and turned eighteen, he probably would have been allowed to spend the last months of his life however he wished.

In our society, children have frequently been treated by pediatricians. While these physicians are especially trained to care for young people, their loyalty and allegiance rest with the parents. Regardless of the youth's age or maturity, the parent is kept fully appraised of the situation and decides on treatment options.

However, recently, things have begun to change somewhat. Adolescent medicine, a new medical subspecialty, has emerged and gained recognition. Many of the practitioners of adolescent medicine were formerly pediatricians or family practice doctors who acquired advanced training in treating teenagers. Most adolescent specialists approach their patients differently than minors are usually dealt with by physicians. Often these doctors inform parents from the start that what occurs between the teenager and themselves will remain confidential. The young patient understands that his parents will only be consulted if he is in physical or emotional danger.

If an adolescent medical specialist had been involved in Juan's case, it is unlikely that he would have recommended the operation over the teen's fervent refusal. Instead, he might have delayed treatment until a compromise could be reached between Juan, his mother, and the surgeons. Although adults making decisions for teenagers may have more seasoned judgment and experience, adolescent medical specialists stress that an adult's perspective often sharply differs from that of a young person. Therefore, these doctors try to afford their youthful patients the same respect and dignity frequently reserved for adults.

Unfortunately, at present, most teenagers continue to be treated by doctors with no genuine expertise in adolescent medicine. While many physician training programs are beginning to appreciate and focus on the unique medical, social, and ethical concerns inherent in treating teens, adolescent medicine still remains a relatively new specialty.

There are other difficulties as well. Perhaps the most obvious are the legal roadblocks involved in medically caring for minors. State laws vary considerably as to when a person can secure his or her own health care and have the last word in any life or death situations that arise. In most states, the young person must be eighteen, but in Alabama a fourteen year old can; in Oregon the teenager has to be fifteen. Nebraska and Wyoming require young people to be nineteen before independently securing health care.

These laws are frequently bent depending on the circumstances involved. A number of states permit minors who are somewhat emancipated such as a teenage mother raising her own child or a young person living alone to be responsible for their own health care decisions. In non-life-threatening situations such as providing older teenage females with gynecological examinations and birth control, doctors may sometimes also treat minors without securing parental consent.

The cost issue is yet another factor in an adolescent's control over his health care. Without the insurance coverage carried by many adults or adequate means to pay a doctor or health care facility, most minors must depend on their parents' or guardians' assistance. While some adolescents may secure treatment at a free clinic or other specially funded facility, they remain unable to see physicians who insist on payment at the close of each office visit.

Any independent decision-making an adolescent achieves in health care will generally vanish if a life-threatening situation occurs. At that point, all control usually reverts back to the teen's parents or guardians. Yet, as in Juan's case, it has been argued that if adults have the right to choose when to die, at times this right should be extended to teenagers.

Those against offering teens the right to choose to die stress that for many young people adolescence is a difficult period characterized by hormonal and emotional upheavals. They feel that frequently a teenager's perceptions and decisions may not be based on a sound rational assessment of the matter at hand but are likely to be influenced by peer pressure, outward appearances, or basic unresolved insecurities. A young person who has not developed a strong capacity for delayed gratification may find it especially difficult to tolerate painful invasive medical procedures that seem endless, but may nevertheless extend his or her life.

These issues are often further complicated by the fact that adolescence tends to be a time of rebellion. Young people poised at an uncomfortable place somewhere between child and adulthood often try out new roles to assert themselves. And when a teenager challenges parental authority in a health care crisis, strong emotions may erupt on both sides.

When, at age fifteen, Kim (not her real name) was diagnosed with cancer, she felt as though her world was about to fall apart. No matter what anyone said, she couldn't stop thinking about her grandmother, who died of the disease when Kim was a small child. She remembered how her parents had set up a hospital bed for Nana in the dining room, so that someone could quickly be at her side when she called for help.

There were countless calls for help as the disease progressed. Kim watched in dismay as she saw the color drain from her grandmother's face and limbs, as the woman's body weight continued to decline.

The girl never forgot her grandmother's trips to the hospital, the barrage of doctors and treatments, and, perhaps worst of all, the elderly woman's horrifying screams when the medication didn't subdue the pain. Although Kim loved her grandmother, she was relieved when the woman who had taught her to read died. Kim never wanted someone who meant so much to her to suffer that way. From the start, there had never been any doubt in the small girl's

*Lester and Joyce Cruzan, parents of
Nancy Beth Cruzan. Ms. Cruzan was a Missouri
woman who went into what her doctors called
an "irreversible vegetative state" as the result
of a car accident. Her parents took their
case to remove her feeding tube all the way
to the United States Supreme Court.*

Karen Ann Quinlan, a New Jersey woman who went into an irreversible coma as the result of ingesting a mixture of alcohol and drugs in 1975. Her fate was debated in one of the most publicized trials in the nation's history.

Joseph and Julia Quinlan, Karen's parents,
filed a petition to have their daughter
taken off life support. Karen was finally
laid to rest in 1986, ten years
after she became comatose.

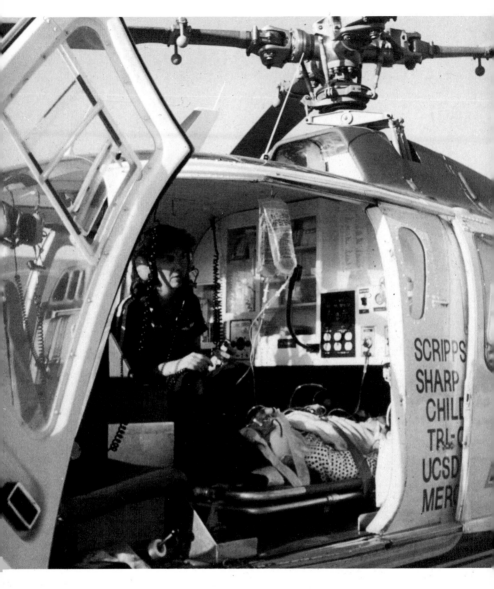

*The advanced technology that has speeded
up response time helps to save lives.
But is it always a good thing?*

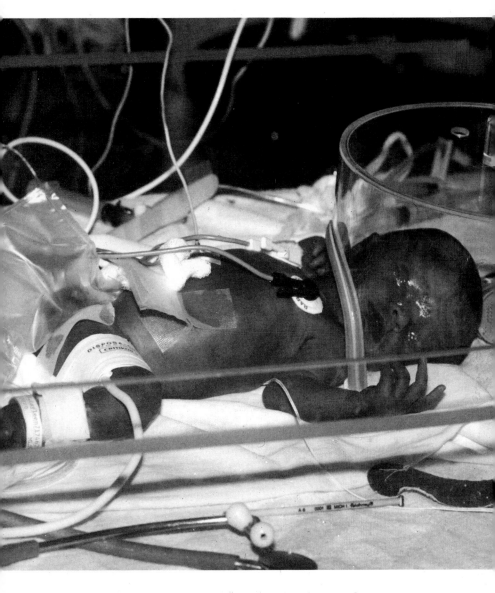

Premature and extremely ill infants who previously would never have survived can now be saved. Many, however, will suffer devastating disabilities.

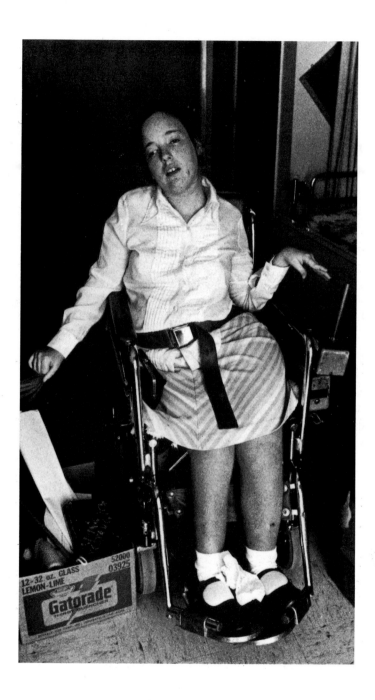

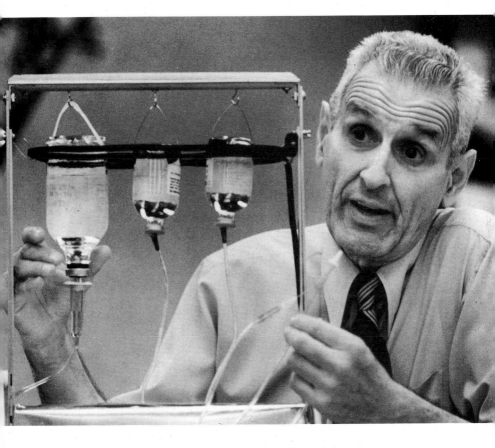

*(Above) Retired Detroit pathologist
Jack Kevorkian, also known as "Dr. Death."
Kevorkian advocates medically assisted
voluntary suicide for very ill patients.
He is shown here with his patient-
activated "suicide device."*

*(Facing page) A young woman with
cerebral palsy and mental retardation.
Will such cases be sacrificed if the right
to die becomes acceptable?*

*New monitoring devices allow us
to keep patients alive longer.*

*It is important for terminally ill patients
to be close to their loved ones as the end
approaches. That way, these patients can make
their wishes known before it's too late
and they can't speak for themselves.*

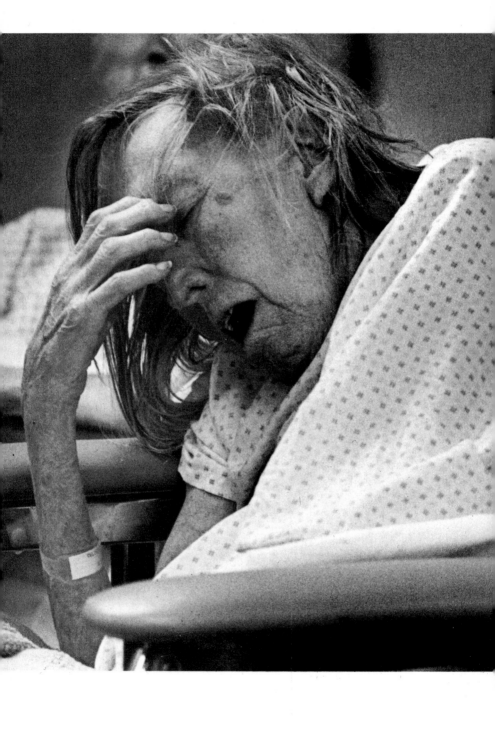

*(Above) Clergy counseling can be
a great comfort to terminally ill patients.*

*(Facing page) Sometimes pain
can be too much to bear.*

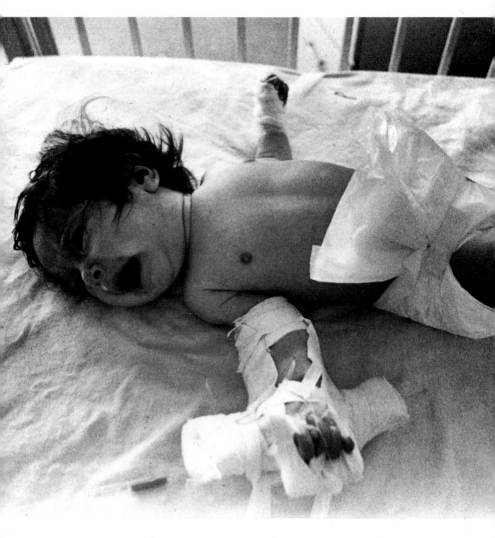

(Above) A baby with AIDS. Will the right to die become a viable alternative in such cases?

(Facing page) Some have argued that our limited funds should go to youngsters with a good chance of recovery rather than to the terminally ill.

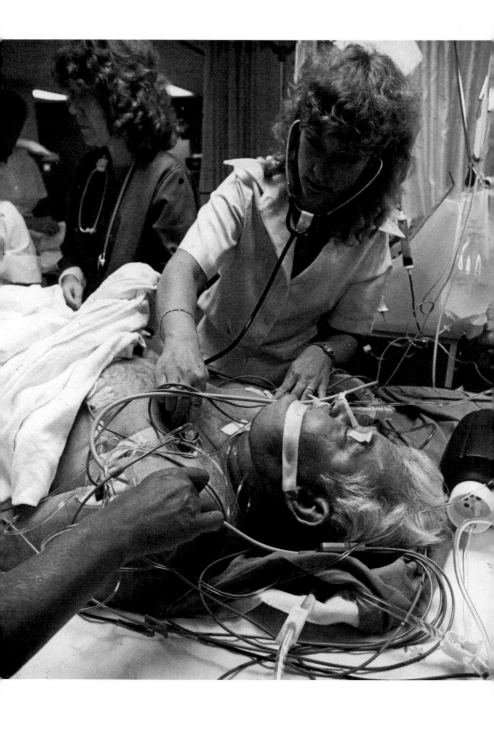

*(Above) Convicted Florida mercy-killer
Roswell Gilbert at a press conference
in 1985. Gilbert said that he was
desperate when he killed his wife,
a victim of Alzheimer's disease,
but that he would do it again.*

(Facing page) The ultimate in machine care

Derek Humphry, founder of the Hemlock Society. Humphry's suicide manual, Final Exit, *hit the top of the best-seller lists.*

Comfort and confidence may be more important than machines.

mind that her grandmother would die. One time she had heard her aunt whisper to her mother, "Cancer is a death sentence." She knew that it had just been a matter of caring for Nana until her time came.

Once Kim was diagnosed with the same disease as her grandmother, she could not shake the dying woman's experiences from her mind. Her doctors and parents tried to convince the teen that her cancer had been detected at an early stage and that her prognosis was favorable. But Kim was too frightened to believe them. Her aunt had said that cancer was a death sentence. It had been for her grandmother, and regardless of what anyone said, Kim felt that she would die of cancer too.

After starting treatment for the disease, there were days when Kim wished she were already dead. Cancer turned her life around in the worst way possible. Her academic and social pursuits were interrupted by her hospital stays. At first Kim didn't want anyone to know she had cancer, but once the word got out, it seemed as though everyone knew. A boy Kim liked since she was twelve (and had hoped to date) even asked her if cancer were catching.

Kim dreaded chemotherapy most. She described her experience:

They told me that chemo would kill the cancer, but sometimes I was sure it was killing me. I'd come home afterwards and throw up for hours. I'd be soaked with sweat and I couldn't stop shaking even when my mother put blankets around me and held me tight. I can't find the words to describe it. It was like World War III started and my body was the battleground. It's funny because at first I was afraid of dying. But after the chemo I used to want to die—anything, just to stop it all.

One day I even grabbed my mother and screamed, "Why don't I die, why don't I just die? Doesn't God know that I can't take anymore?" My mother started to cry and later I felt bad that I did that to her. But I couldn't help it. My life was a mess and I was a walking sack of pain.

In addition to the intense physical discomfort, Kim also had to contend with patches of her hair falling out and her skin taking on a sallow tint at a point when she had been contemplating a career in modeling. She also fell seriously behind in her schoolwork and felt that with the exception of a few people, her friends had been more frightened than supportive.

Fortunately, Kim's cancer went into remission, and in many ways her life is now like any teenager's. The hair she thought was gone forever is long and lustrous again, she's doing well in school, and she's dating a boy who was helpful to her following her recovery.

Kim is glad she survived and pleased with how things turned out. But her mother vividly remembers a period when her daughter's outlook had taken a darker turn. As she recalled:

There were times when it was rough going for all of us. I watched my mother die of cancer and couldn't bear to see the same thing happen to my only child. Kim's prognosis had been considerably better from the start, but I couldn't in good conscience make her any promises about recovery. Even the doctors could only hope for the best.

There were moments when Kim wanted to stop everything and give up. She knew that without chemotherapy she didn't have a chance, but sometimes she didn't want that chance—it didn't seem worth what she had to go through.

My husband and I assured Kim that these feelings would pass. We told her that her fear and discomfort were affecting her judgment, but deep inside I knew that my daughter had a valid point. Sometimes I ask myself how I'd feel if Kim hadn't recovered and I'd made her go through all that. There were days when she'd scream and beg my husband and I not to take her for chemotherapy. But we stood firm. We told her she was too young to have a say in these matters and forced her into the car. I feel justified in what I did because, despite counseling, Kim was too depressed at the time to see the situation clearly. But then I have to remind myself that it was my daughter not me who physically suffered. And even though I'm glad that I made her do what needed to be done, if her cancer returned, I am not sure I could do it again.

Kim's mother attributes her attitude to having a daughter with cancer, but most parents would not afford their offspring the right to die. This may be at least partly due to their legal and ethical obligations as well as the pain inherent in losing a child. Nevertheless, some medical facilities have moved toward further involving minors in health care decisions. For example, a teenager with cancer may still not have the final say in whether he or she will undergo chemotherapy, but the young person may be given a voice in where the treatments will take place.

Adolescent medical specialists believe that allowing teenagers to have a say in their treatment enhances their feelings of being in control as well as makes distasteful medical or surgical procedures easier to tolerate. Society has also begun to move away slightly from treating children and teenagers as mere extensions of their parents. The first legal decision that gave young people a foothold on independent medical choice was the 1976 Supreme Court case of *Carey, Governor of New York et al* v. *Population Services International et al.* Regarding a teenager's right to contraception, the justices wrote, "Constitutional rights do not mature magically at adulthood."[2] However, no court has upheld an adolescent's right to die and the Supreme Court has already specified that living wills are invalid for minors.

Right-to-die opponents stress that extending this option to teens is unthinkable. They feel that adolescents lack the maturity and judgment to override parental concerns. Many right-to-die advocates agree with them, firmly believing that life or death decisions must be reserved for clear-thinking adults. Yet at times gravely ill teenagers acquire a wisdom far beyond their chronological years, and there are those who believe their right to die is as valid as someone's a few years older.

6 ᐧᐯᐢᐩᐧᐯᐢᐩ

Final Choices

D avid Rivlin was a thirty-eight-year-old quadri-plegic from Michigan who, for over three years, had been bedridden at the Oak Hill Care Center near Detroit. He mostly spent his days and eve-nings listening to talk on the radio or, when an at-tendant raised his bed, watching TV. The rest of the time he studied the room he was unable to leave—going over every detail of the ceiling, walls, furniture, and draperies. It wasn't the life he had dreamed about. Most of the time, he felt it wasn't a life at all.

Rivlin's physical problems stemmed from a swimming accident he had when he was twenty years old. On August 10, 1971, he and a girlfriend were ocean bathing when Rivlin was caught in the undertow and thrown head first into the sand. He lost consciousness momentarily, but seconds later he saw his hand floating in front of his face and realized that he couldn't feel anything. Rivlin knew he had broken his neck.

Nearby swimmers carried the young man to shore. They saved his life, but unfortunately Rivlin was paralyzed, except for some minor arm and upper body movement. It was difficult for him to cope with what happened. One moment he felt as though his whole life were ahead of him, and the next everything he valued was gone. For weeks Rivlin felt enraged, but afterwards he became depressed and despondent. He lost his appetite and dropped nearly sixty pounds.

Three years later, in 1974, David Rivlin decided to try to piece his life back together. He enrolled at Oakland University in Michigan where he lived and studied, assisted by a nursing aide. He often suffered from colds and infections, and frequently had to be hospitalized. Nevertheless, the young man continued his studies until 1979 when the paralysis spread to his arms.

Needing full-time care, Rivlin entered a nursing home in Dearborn, Michigan. There he fell in love with a staff member and, despite his medical problems, the two planned to marry. But the wedding never came about. Once the couple became engaged, Rivlin moved in with his fiancée and pressures resulting from his condition destroyed the relationship. The pair broke up and Rivlin became a permanent resident at still another nursing home.

In 1986 he was operated on for a spinal aneurysm that doctors believed had sped up his paralysis. But the surgery was unsuccessful, and several months later, when he could no longer breathe on his own, Rivlin was put on a respirator. Connected by a hose to a hole in his throat, David Rivlin couldn't escape the continuous whir of the machine keeping him alive.

More frustrated than ever by his helplessness, the once outgoing young man became increasingly withdrawn. He abandoned his former pastimes of reading and listening to classical music and before long announced that he wanted to die. He simply told his family and friends that he didn't wish to continue in his present condition.

However, his physician flatly refused to unplug his respirator. Realizing that he would need a court order to die, in May 1989 Rivlin filed a petition with the Oakland County Circuit Court. On July 5 Judge Hilda R. Gage granted Rivlin's request that as a competent adult he had the right to refuse medical treatment.

About two weeks later, David Rivlin was taken to a friend's home where he enjoyed a delicious meal of his favorite Mexican foods. The medical director of a Michigan hospice then administered a sufficient dose of valium and morphine to render Rivlin unconscious so he would feel no discomfort at the end. The respirator was turned off, and with his closest friends at his side, David Rivlin died.

In accordance with Rivlin's wishes, classical music was played, wine was served, and Hebrew prayers were said. Before dying, Rivlin claimed that he hadn't had second thoughts about what he was doing. He said that dying meant he would finally be able to rest in peace.

While his supporters argued that Rivlin had a right not to have to live on a respirator, some health officials were upset by the court's acceptance of the young man's choice. They felt that the highly publicized incident set a poor example for other disabled individuals who might be better off striving for a meaningful existence than killing themselves.

As they had anticipated, another case made headlines less than two months later when Larry McAfee, a Georgia quadriplegic, also petitioned a court to have his respirator turned off. McAfee had been a civil engineer with a genuine zeal for the outdoors. An avid sportsman, he had fished, hunted, and played baseball. But that was before he was paralyzed in a motorcycle accident.

In an emotionally moving hearing, McAfee told the judge how he awakened every morning "fearful of each new day." He added, "There is nothing I have found or can think of that I really enjoy or that has helped my situation."[1] Like David Rivlin, Larry McAfee's suit was successful—the judge recognized his right to die.

Since that time, a number of cases similar to Rivlin's and McAfee's have reached the courts. But even though the right-to-die debate often centers around the use of life supports, some people feel this right should extend to any severely ill or disabled individual who wishes to end his or her life. Proponents of this view condone resorting to suicide or legalized euthanasia (mercy killing) in these instances.

Those are the sentiments of Joel K., a twenty-six-year-old San Francisco artist, who was just gaining recognition in his field when he learned he was HIV positive. A year later, he had a full-blown case of AIDS. Taking AZT while under a doctor's care, Joel tried to live his life to the fullest. Between battling illnesses and infections, he painted as well as kept in close touch with his friends and family. Nevertheless, within eleven months, he lost nearly fifty pounds and became extremely weak.

Joel had always been a proud, independent person and it was important to him to remain in control of his life. Knowing that he had a fatal disease from which no one had recovered, Joel wanted to be able to decide when he was going to "call it quits." After visiting a number of doctors, he managed to accumulate a sufficient stash of narcotics and barbiturates to enable him to die painlessly in his sleep.

Joel knows that when the time comes he will have to take the pills himself. He has specified that he's to be alone then since he doesn't want his loved ones to be legally implicated in his death. Although Joel is frequently in a great deal of pain, at the time of this writing, he still clung to life. He said that he has "too many good days" to die yet, but he knows that one day he'll feel differently.

A considerable number of others agree with this view. Some individuals also feel that physicians should actively assist in the process if asked to. According to Derek Humphry, a founder of the Hemlock Society (a group that advocates "self-deliverance" under certain circumstances), "Part of good medicine is to help you out of this life as well as help you in. When care is no longer possible and the patient seeks relief from euthanasia, the help of physicians is most appropriate."[2]

Humphry, an English journalist, emigrated to the United States in 1978 and began The National Hemlock Society two years later. This nonprofit national organization stands by the following four principles:

1. Hemlock acts to positively influence public opinion in support of "the rights of people who are terminally ill to end their own lives in a planned manner."
2. Hemlock does not condone suicide for individuals who are not terminally ill. It is against suicide for emotional or financial reasons and applauds the work of suicide prevention centers in this realm.
3. Hemlock stresses that "the final decision to terminate life is ultimately one's own. . . . [It] believes this action and most of all its timing, to be an extremely personal decision, wherever possible taken

in concert with family, close friends, and personal physician."
4. Hemlock does not wish to impose its views on anyone who doesn't share its beliefs and respects the differing opinions of various religions and philosophies.[3]

In many respects Derek Humphry practices what he preaches. He helped three family members contending with extreme pain and debilitation to end their lives: a brother on mechanical life supports as well as a terminally ill wife and father-in-law. He believes, however, that "justifiable suicide" or "rational and planned self-deliverance" should be carried out only within the parameters defined below:

1. "The person is a mature adult." Although the individual's age may vary, Humphry feels this alternative is inappropriate for children and young adults.
2. "The person has clearly made a considered decision." Humphry advises an individual contemplating suicide to leave tangible proof of his or her views on the matter beforehand through a living will or other advance directives for health care.
3. "The self-deliverance has not been made at the first knowledge of the life-threatening illness, and reasonable medical help has been sought." This is important to ensure that the person is not responding irrationally and has had time to carefully think things out.
4. "The treating physician has been informed and his or her response has been taken into account." Humphry notes that this conversation is important for clarification in case the patient misheard or misunderstood the diagnosis or ramifications of the disease.

5. "The person has made a will disposing of his or her worldly effects."
6. "The person has made plans to exit this life that do not involve others in criminal liability." Committing suicide is not illegal, but in some states assisting in a suicide is. Therefore, Humphry stresses that the individual must take his or her own life—a friend or relative should not administer lethal drugs, release poisonous fumes, or otherwise directly help.
7. "The person leaves a note saying exactly why he or she is committing suicide." Humphry acknowledges that some people choose to die in a hotel or motel to shield their families from the trauma of finding their body. In these instances, he feels that ". . . one should leave a note of apology to the staff for inconvenience and embarrassment caused."[4]

In recent years, Derek Humphry has emerged as a vocal figure in the right-to-die movement. Although he has published a number of books, he became especially prominent as a result of his highly controversial text, *Final Exit,* a clearly written suicide manual providing instructions on how to kill oneself with a minimum of discomfort and complications. This dangerously informative work contains data on mixing lethal dosages of prescription drugs, as well as helpful hints for effectively using a plastic bag or auto exhaust to asphyxiate oneself.

As skyrocketing sales propelled the book to the top of the *New York Times* best seller list, right-to-life advocates and others loudly condemned the practical nature of Humphry's guide to dying. Despite its popularity, even some book dealers declined to sell it. That was how the owner of a Grand Rapids, Michigan, bookstore felt. She explained: "My father was a doctor, and my brother is a doctor. I was raised in an atmosphere of caring for life and saving life. My sales staff felt the same way. They said they could not put such a book in a customer's hands when they didn't know how it would be used."[5]

Humphry supporters feel that the author provided an important service in supplying needed hands-on information for people living with prolonged and debilitating illnesses. The author also appeared on a variety of television talk shows to both promote and defend his widely selling book. He insisted that, "People want to take control of their dying. My book is a sort of insurance, a comforter there on the bookshelf that they could make their escape from this world if they were suffering unbearably."[6]

Yet many people remained concerned that the book could be used for unintended purposes. They questioned whether the specific information offered on lethal doses of medications might not facilitate difficult-to-detect homicides. Although the text urges emotionally troubled individuals to seek psychiatric help, there is always the danger that the reader might forgo the counseling in favor of following the suicide formulas.

This is what Ethel Adelman claimed happened to her twenty-nine-year-old son Adrian, who committed suicide in September 1991 after reading *Final Exit*. Adrian, who had suffered from recurring depression for a number of months, heard about Humphry's book and ordered a copy for himself. When the book arrived, Mrs. Adelman, fearing its effect on her troubled son, hid it in a closet. But her efforts didn't help—Adrian simply went out and bought another copy.

Unfortunately, the young man became obsessed with the manual. Although he had been in therapy for depression, and had shown signs of improvement, after reading *Final Exit,* he avoided treatment. His brother Alan described what happened this way: "It *[Final Exit]* showed him the way. He wanted it to be a nonpainful way. The book was clearly the answer to his dilemma of how to commit suicide without feeling any pain. He said he would never shoot himself or do anything like that. Everybody tried to help him, but when he got his hands on the book, he was no longer interested in psychiatric help or therapy."[7]

While the Adelmans were concerned about the book's effect on Adrian, they didn't realize how serious the problem was until it was too late. On Sunday evening September 1, 1991, Adrian's mother, aunt, and uncle arrived at the young man's apartment to pick him up for dinner. They had looked forward to spending a pleasant evening with Adrian, but instead found him lying dead in the hallway with a plastic bag over his head. After going through his belongings, the police found his hoard of prescription drugs along with a copy of *Final Exit.*

Ethel Adelman blames her son's death on Humphry's book, which she feels has potentially disastrous consequences for society. She said, "I think he [Adrian] would still be here today if it weren't for this book." Adrian's brother Alan added, "He would still be suffering and suicidal, but the book certainly facilitated his death. The book took away his life."[8]

Not everyone feels the way the Adelmans do about right-to-die aids such as Derek Humphry's book. NBC correspondent Betty Rollins wrote the introduction to Humphry's book, and her role in assisting her terminally ill mother to die is well known. Ms. Rollins was the only child of Ida Rollins, an Eastern European immigrant known for her dynamic, vibrant personality. Ms. Rollins recalls how every day after school, the neighborhood children flocked to their house to savor her mother's tasty snacks. Everyone loved Ida and people of all ages seemed drawn to her.

Through the years, Ida Rollins was a tremendous source of strength and fortitude for her family. When, in 1973, Betty was operated on for breast cancer, her mother refused to leave her bedside. Mrs. Rollins's upbeat, take-charge attitude was instrumental in her daughter's recovery, but, unfortunately, less than a decade later, Mrs. Rollins was diagnosed with ovarian cancer herself. She showed no fear or self-pity while enduring the chemotherapy sessions, which left her weak and exhausted. Instead, she survived, and within eight months resumed many of the everyday activities she had been forced to give up earlier.

Mrs. Rollins joyously celebrated her seventy-fifth birthday with her daughter and son-in-law, but unfortunately her cancer spread, and in June 1983 she resumed chemotherapy. Mrs. Rollins knew it would be a difficult ordeal, but she very much wanted to live. However, the treatments proved too much for her and after just two sessions, the doctors said they couldn't continue them.

At that juncture, Ida Rollins's prospects looked bleak. The doctors were unable to operate, and the malignant tumor continued to grow. She was in a great deal of pain and at times couldn't eat or swallow. Mrs. Rollins finally confided to her daughter that after having enjoyed a wonderful life, she was ready to die.

At first, Betty Rollins didn't want to accept what she heard. She hoped her mother was just feeling sad and would cheer up the following day. But that never happened. Although Ida Rollins loved living, she felt that advanced cancer had reduced her days to suffering. She was prepared to take her own life, but since she didn't know how to proceed, she asked her daughter for help.

Once she realized that her mother was sincere, Ms. Rollins was determined not to disappoint her. But the dilemma of finding a painless way for a dignified woman to die remained. Ms. Rollins and her husband ruled out carbon monoxide poisoning because they didn't own a car, and arsenic and cyanide poison were out of the question since these substances weren't readily available. Feeling that she had to quickly find a way to alleviate her mother's distress, Betty Rollins even contemplated securing a gun from a street gang she had done a news story on. However, knowing that her mother wouldn't want to die violently, Ms. Rollins instead grew more determined than ever to find an acceptable alternative.

She knew that she needed to identify the types and dosages of prescription drugs that would enable her mother to pass away peacefully, but here she met a roadblock. Ms. Rollins confided her concerns to doctors and pharmacists, but they refused to help. Even when she pretended that her inquiries were for a news report, she was still unable to learn what she needed to know.

Finally, a close friend put her in touch with a doctor in Europe who supported euthanasia and viewed helping Ida Rollins to take her own life as a humane gesture. He told Betty Rollins which drug combinations would be most effective for her purpose. Armed with this knowledge, Ida Rollins took charge of her death the way she had run her life. Making certain that her finances and household affairs were in order, she stoically chose October 17, 1983, as the day to die. It was extremely important to her to act while she was still able to help herself.

On that October evening, her daughter and son-in-law stood supportively at her bedside as she swallowed the pills. When Mrs. Rollins drifted off to sleep, a neighbor came to sit with her so that her daughter and her husband could leave. After weeks of trying to be brave and supportive and hold up, Betty Rollins broke down sobbing. She knew she would always miss her mother, but she was grateful that she had been able to help grant Ida Rollins's last wish.

Two years later, in 1985, Betty Rollins lost a second breast to cancer. She claims that although she hopes to die peacefully in her sleep when she's ninety, she still supports the right of terminally ill individuals to take their own lives. Ms. Rollins was never prosecuted for assisting in her mother's suicide, although technically she could have been. While passive euthanasia—withdrawing a respirator or feeding tube—has gained a significant degree of acceptance in medical, legal, and religious circles, active euthanasia—playing an aggressive role in ending another person's life—remains controversial. The American Medical Association looks disparagingly on it, laws forbid it, and religious groups are opposed to it.

The issue of physician-assisted suicide recently gained notoriety due to retired Detroit pathologist Jack Kevorkian, also known as "Dr. Death." Kevorkian, who has sometimes been described as a "serial mercy killer," advocates "medicide," or medically assisted voluntary suicide for very ill patients who desire it. To facilitate the process, Kevorkian created a "suicide device," which he described as simulating what "we do now with legal executions, except with the device the person does it himself by pushing a button."[9]

Kevorkian's work first came to the public's attention in June 1990 when he helped Janet Adkins, a fifty-four-year-old woman suffering from Alzheimer's disease, to take her own life. Alzheimer's disease is a progressive degenerative illness that erodes the victim's mind and eventually prevents the person from performing even basic tasks. When she approached Kevorkian, Ms. Adkins, a part-time English and piano teacher, could no longer spell or read music.

"She told me she wanted to take her own life while she was still clear in her mind and knew what she was doing," Kevorkian explained, describing the circumstances surrounding Adkins's death. "It's not a matter of how long you live, but the quality of life you live, and it was her life and her decision to choose. She made that decision based upon the fact that the things she loved most—reading, literature, music—and all that she couldn't do anymore." [10]

The suicide took place in a van at a Michigan campground. The doctor later expressed his regret at having had to rent a campsite, but he stressed that clinics, churches, and funeral homes refuse to allow the procedure. He added that he hoped the incident would "kick the medical profession into action."

To begin the suicide, Kevorkian attached a heart monitor to Adkins and inserted an intravenous tube in her arm which allowed a harmless saline solution to flow into her body. When she felt ready, Ms. Adkins pushed a button, releasing a drug that caused her to lose consciousness. Moments later, a dose of potassium chloride emitted from the machine stopped her heart. Dr. Kevorkian reported that she drifted into unconsciousness within seconds and died about six minutes later. He described her death as being "like a painless heart attack in a deep sleep."

After she expired, Kevorkian notified the police. He explained that he only agreed to assist Ms.

Adkins after an experimental drug maintenance program he urged her to try had failed. He underscored the fact that he would never accept a fee to assist in a suicide, and stated that he might one day use his "suicide device" himself if he became hopelessly ill.

Kevorkian was charged with first degree murder for his role in Janet Adkins's death. He expected to be prosecuted, but the charges were later dropped since there was no Michigan state law expressly prohibiting assisted suicide. But even though a judge warned him not to do it again, Kevorkian helped two other women commit suicide in the Fall of 1991.

This time, fifty-three-year-old Sherry Miller, who had multiple sclerosis, and Mary Wantz, who, at fifty-eight, suffered from an excruciatingly painful pelvic disease, had approached the physician for help. Wantz underwent ten operations for her illness and had been homebound for three years. Despite extensive medication and treatment, her neighbors noted that the woman's screams of pain frequently awakened them during the night. Now with her husband at her side for comfort, Ms. Wantz, like Ms. Adkins, received a lethal drug dose and died shortly thereafter.

Sherry Miller, once an outstanding swimmer and skater, was confined to a wheelchair after losing the use of much of her body. Although she was not in pain, Ms. Miller felt her life was too diminished for her to want to continue. Since her veins weren't strong enough to use Kevorkian's suicide machine, a face mask attached to a canister of carbon monoxide was used. The two women died at approximately the same time in a rented cabin in Michigan's Bald Mountain Recreation area. When it was over, once again Kevorkian called the police—this time to report the double "doctor-assisted suicide."

The county prosecutor conducted an investigation and Dr. Kevorkian was subsequently charged with two counts of murder. While out on bail awaiting trial, Jack Kevorkian was linked to still another suicide. This time the patient was Susan Williams, a fifty-two year-old woman who had gone blind and become severely debilitated as the result of multiple sclerosis.

Kevorkian stated that while he counseled Williams and was present at the time of her death, he did not actively assist her in using carbon monoxide to commit suicide. According to the doctor's lawyer, Geoffrey Fieger, "Her life for all intents and purposes was meaningless. She was the person who put the mask on her face. She was the person who turned on the can of carbon monoxide. She was the person who ended her own life without the aid of anyone whatsoever."[11]

Dr. Kevorkian still feels that medically assisted suicide is crucial to the critically ill, and on November 23, 1992, he helped a sixth person to die. This time it was Catherine Andreyev, a forty-six-year-old cancer-striken woman. Then on December 15, 1992, Kevorkian assisted in the suicides of two more chronically ill women who had been in a great deal of pain. Following their deaths he helped several others to kill themselves. Although the previous murder charges against Kevorkian were dropped, a bill has since been signed into law making it illegal in Michigan to assist in a suicide. However, Kevorkian insists that he will continue his work even if sent to jail for his actions.

Jack Kevorkian's radical views have frequently clashed with those of the general medical community and even segments of the right-to-die movement. Many right-to-die proponents stress the importance of careful safeguards in ending a human life. Kevorkian has been criticized for failing to secure second opinions, consent forms, and psychiatric exams for his patients. Even the Hemlock Society expressed some dismay over the doctor's actions, since he willingly assists in the suicides of patients who are not terminally ill.

While Kevorkian may not be highly regarded, a small group of other physicians also contends that under some circumstances, doctors should help their patients die. They insist that such measures should only be implemented if the patients have carefully determined that this is what they want. Those favoring physician-assisted suicide believe that terminally ill people have a right to such help. They stress that doctors know far better than anyone else how to help us die painlessly and with dignity.

Opponents of physician-assisted suicide feel that a physician who kills, even upon request, distorts the ends of medicine and erodes trust in the profession. They also maintain that the hospital physician on duty when the patient asks to die might not be the patient's doctor and therefore would not be in a position to assess whether the patient's decision is consistent with the rest of his or her life. Those against physician-assisted suicide further argue that doctors already have too much power over us to take on additional authority by assisting in suicides.

Nevertheless, a 1992 public opinion poll indicated that 81 percent of those surveyed agreed with the concept of medically-assisted suicide. Active euthanasia is already aggressively practiced in the Netherlands, where over 7,000 terminally ill and disabled individuals annually die that way. Although euthanasia is technically illegal there, Dutch authorities will not take action against physicians involved in mercy killings if they notify coroners of their actions as well as follow certain procedures.

Some serious questions regarding this procedure have arisen, though. A recent study indicated that Dutch hospital and physician statistics are somewhat hazy on the precise number of euthanized patients and whether these deaths are always confined to competent, terminally ill patients who ask to die. Instead, the research revealed that at least every sixth or seventh euthanasia case in the Netherlands is not "physician-assisted suicide, but homicide—approved by no one and reported to no one."[12]

Dr. Carlos Gomez, author of the book *Regulating Death: Euthanasia and the Case of the Netherlands,* expressed his concerns about physician-assisted suicide as follows: "My fear is that euthanasia [in the United States] would be used as it sometimes is in Holland, as a tool of social and economic control. Poor people, especially in this country where we deny medical services to many of them, are the most vulnerable to be euthanized."[13]

The legalization of euthanasia has already been placed on the ballot in some areas. On November 5, 1991, Washington state residents voted on Initiative 119, known as the Death with Dignity proposal. The initiative supported the right of terminally ill patients to commit suicide, assisted by their physicians, as well as clarified the circumstances under which life supports could be withdrawn from patients who specified that intent in a living will. Some medical experts were concerned that if the bill passed, suicidal individuals might flock to Washington, where unethical, profit-minded physicians might set up practices to meet the demand. Washington's Initiative 119 was defeated, but the momentum behind the issue remained. A similar bill was voted down in California in November 1992.

Regardless of the outcome on these and other future referendums, it is clear that the right to die is no longer a taboo topic, but instead has evolved into a mainstream societal concern around which the ongoing debate continues. In reaffirming its opposition to euthanasia or physician-assisted suicide, the American Medical Association stated, "Medicine is a profession dedicated to healing. Its tools should not be used to kill people."[14] Yet a sizable segment of our society disagrees with this assessment. Perhaps their feelings were best expressed by a Unitarian minister, Reverend Marvin Evans, when he said, "Death is not the enemy. Death is part of life. People want control over their lives, and this is the final and perhaps most important thing in a life."[15]

Epilogue

The right to die remains controversial on an ethical, legal, and social level. Precise, tangible conclusions are difficult to come by when evaluating an issue that often varies dramatically from case to case as well as touches on the personal belief systems of so many individuals. While present-day trends reflect prevailing attitudes, these have been known to change. Some people argue that court decisions and ballot referendums cannot alter deep-rooted feelings about life and death. Perhaps ultimately, the decision to acknowledge or ever act on the right to die will always be an extremely personal one.

Appendix
Organizations Concerned
With the Right To Die

American Coalition for
Life
P.O. Box 44415
Ft. Washington, Maryland
20749
202-466-8630

American Life Lobby
P.O. Box 490
Stafford, Virginia 22554
703-659-9171

Center for the Rights of
the Terminally Ill
2319 18th Avenue S
Fargo, North Dakota
58103
701-237-5667

Choice in Dying
200 Varick Street
New York, New York
10014
212-366-5540

National Hemlock Society
P.O. Box 11830
Eugene, Oregon 97440-
3900
503-342-5748

National Right to Life
419 Seventh Street NW
Suite 500
Washington, D.C. 20004
202-626-8800

Medical Ethics:
Hastings Center
255 Elm Road
Briarcliff Manor, New
York 10510
914-762-8500

Park Ridge Center
676 N. St. Clair, Suite 450
Chicago, Illinois 60611
312-266-2222

Source Notes

Chapter 1

1. Sharon Begley, "Choosing Death," *Newsweek* (August 26, 1991):43.
2. *Ibid.*
3. *Ibid,* p. 44.
4. Donahue, "Should Doctors Decide Who Lives?" Transcript #2913 (March 29, 1990).
5. *Ibid.*
6. Katherine Ames, "Last Rights," *Newsweek* (August 26, 1991):40.
7. *Ibid.*
8. *Ibid.*
9. Milton D. Heifetz, *The Right To Die* (New York, G. P. Putnam's Sons, 1975) p. 185.
10. Ames, *op. cit.,* p. 41.
11. *Ibid.*
12. Ted Gest, "Changing the Rules in Dying," *U.S. News & World Report* (July 9, 1990):24.
13. "Back From the Dead," *Time* (October 6, 1986):35.
14. Ted Gest, "Is There a Right To Die?" *U.S. News & World Report* (December 11, 1989):36.

Chapter 2
1. B. D. Colen, *Karen Ann Quinlan: Dying in the Age of Eternal Life* (New York: Nash Publishing, 1976) p. 37.
2. *Ibid.,* p. 31.
3. *Ibid.,* p. 55.
4. *Ibid.,* p. 43.
5. Alain L. Sanders, "Whose Right to Die?" *Time* (December 11, 1989):80.
6. John M. Swomley, "The Cruzan Decision: Refusing Treatment," *The Christian Century* (November 29, 1989):1110.
7. Nancy Gibbs, "Love and Let Die," *Time* (March 19, 1990):64.
8. Sanders, *op. cit.*
9. Linda Greenhouse, "Family's Request to End Feeding of Woman in Coma Is Denied," *The New York Times* (June 26, 1990):A19.
10. *Ibid.,* p. A18.
11. "Right to Die Case; Woman's Fight Is Over," *New York Post* (January 7, 1991):11.
12. *Ibid.*
13. "The Next Cruzan Case," *U.S. News & World Report* (January 14, 1991):8.

Chapter 3
1. Joseph Carey, "The Faulty Promise of Living Wills," *U.S. News & World Report* (July 24, 1989):63.
2. Robert J. Klein, "Why Everyone Should Write a Living Will," *Money* (June 1989):165.
3. Carey, *op cit.*

Chapter 4
1. Jeff Lyon, *Playing God in the Nursery* (New York: W. W. Norton & Company, 1985) p. 27.
2. *Ibid.,* p. 33.
3. *Ibid.,* p. 35.
4. B.D. Cohen, *Hard Choices: Mixed Blessings of Modern Medical Technology.* (New York: G.P. Putnam's Sons, 1986) p. 193.

5. *Ibid.*, p. 177.
6. Jeff Lyon, pp. 190–91.
7. *Ibid.*

Chapter 5
1. Nancy Dubler, Esq. and David Nimmons, *Ethics on Call: A Medical Ethicist Shows How to Take Charge of Life and Death Choices* (New York: Harmony Books, 1992) p. 286.
2. U.S. Supreme Court Reports, vol. 52 Lawyers' Edition 20, p. 625.

Chapter 6
1. "Death Wish," *Time* (September 18, 1989):67.
2. William A. Henry III, "Do It Yourself Death Lessons," *Time* (August 19, 1991):55.
3. The National Hemlock Society, organization circular, 1992.
4. Derek Humphrey, "The Case for Rational Suicide," *Suicide and Life-Threatening Behavior* (Winter 1987):335–36.
5. Henry III, *op. cit.*
6. *Ibid.*
7. Bonnie Angelo, "Assiging the Blame for a Young Man's Suicide," *Time* (November 18, 1991):16.
8. *Ibid.*
9. "MD Helps Patient Use Suicide Machine," *The Star Ledger* (June 6, 1990):11.
10. *Ibid.*
11. "Suicide Doc Linked to Death of 4th Woman," *New York Post* (May 16, 1992):4.
12. John Leo, "Cozy Little Homicides," *U.S. News & World Report* (November 11, 1991):28.
13. Timothy Egan, "Washington Voters Weigh Aid of Doctors in Suicide," *The New York Times* (October 14, 1991):A20.
14. *Ibid.*
15. *Ibid.*, p. A1.

For Further Reading

Articles:

Brack, Barbara. "Rational Suicide: My Mother's Story," *The Christian Century* (November 13, 1991):1054–55.

Denizen, Norman K. "The Suicide Machine," *Society* (July–August 1992):7–10.

Gibbs, Nancy. "Dr. Death Strikes Again," *Time* (November 4, 1991):78.

Goode, Erica E. "Defending the Right to Die," *U.S. News & World Report* (September 30, 1991):38.

Lawton, Kim A. "The Doctor as an Executioner," *Christianity Today* (December 16, 1991):50–52.

Markson, Elizabeth. "Moral Dilemmas," *Society* (July–August 1992):4–6.

Rosenbaum, Ron. "The Trial of the Suicide Doctor," *Vanity Fair* (May 1991):146–151.

Seltzer, Richard. "A Question of Mercy," *The New York Times Magazine* (September 22, 1991):32–33.

Books:

Craig, Jean. *Between Hello and Goodbye: A Man and Woman's Struggle for Dignity Against Disease and an Unresponsive Medical Establishment.* New York: St. Martin's Press, 1991.

Flanders, Stephen. *Suicide.* New York: Facts On File, 1991.

Fradin, Dennis Brindell. *Medicine: Yesterday, Today and Tomorrow*. Chicago: Childrens Press, 1989.

Gay, Kathlyn. *Church and State: Government and Religion in the United States*. Brookfield, Connecticut: Millbrook Press, 1992.

Hyde, Margaret O., and Elizabeth H. Forsyth. *Suicide*. New York: Franklin Watts, 1991.

Jussim, David. *Medical Ethics*. Englewood Cliffs, New Jersey: Silver Burdett, 1990.

Kevorkian, Jack. *Prescription Medicide: The Goodness of a Planned Death*. Buffalo, New York: Prometheus, 1991.

Lieberson, Alan D. *The Living Will Handbook: The Right to Decide Your Own Fate*. New York: Hastings House, 1991.

Menten, Ted. *Gentle Closings: How to Say Goodbye to Someone You Love*. Philadelphia: Running Press, 1992.

Smith, Bradley E., and Jess M. Brallier. *Write Your Own Living Will*. New York: Crown, 1991.

Thomasma, David C., and Glenn Graber. *Euthanasia: Toward an Ethical Social Policy*. New York: HarperCollins, 1990.

Index